"What a timely book for this current crisis! With her characteristic wit and wisdom, Teresa Tomeo holds before our eyes powerful witnesses of men, women, and children who are responding to the current pandemic in a way that is sure to inspire us to do similar things."

—Fr. John Riccardo
Executive Director of Acts XXIX

"The fact that Teresa was able to create this resource even while she was grieving the loss of her mother proves that she practices what she preaches. She shows how God didn't cause this health crisis, but He allows it so we can help reveal Him to the world. Thus, she underscores the need for us to not let fear overcome our lives, and she gives examples of how obstacles can become opportunities for a stronger relationship with God and each other. Based on real statistics, she gives us a road map on what to do during this time of isolation, pointing to some great examples we can all learn from. That is why I, and so many others, admire her work. This collection of wisdom and spiritual riches from our Catholic heritage will be a welcome gift in this time of pandemic."

—Fr. Chris Alar, MIC
Director of the Association of Marian Helpers

"What a beautiful guide to the great spiritual reawakening we must lead by the way we live our lives! This coronavirus time is not about coronavirus so much as it is about our spiritual viruses of lukewarmness and indifference. Pope Francis often talks about how we go through life anesthetized. No more! We cannot afford to. Not if we believe in Jesus Christ! Not if we know His love for us and the truth of what His Resurrection promises! Teresa Tomeo has put together a helpful guide to get and keep us on a road to true conversion. And what a beautiful tribute to her beloved mother and her life of faith!"

—Kathryn Jean Lopez
Senior Fellow, National Review Institute and
Editor-at-Large, *National Review*

"A timely book that addresses our fears using our faith to help us successfully cope with the current crisis. All people of Christian faiths will benefit from this book. Effective and interesting research with facts that guide us during these turbulent times. What is most powerful about this book is the prayers, which give you hope and confidence!"

—Susan Tassone
Author of *Jesus Speaks to Faustina and You*

"The saints and the Scriptures, as well as modern therapists, have a lot to say about fear of death and anxiety over money. These are also the twin worries associated with coronavirus. In *Conquering Coronavirus: How Faith Can Put Your Fears to Rest*, Teresa Tomeo shows us how Christ's Body, the Church, has endured many such threats throughout her history and how we can learn from our collective experience. In a brisk, personal style, she gathers data and lists resources, collects relevant testimonies, and encourages us to not just to endure this moment but to embrace and grow through it. We all know or will know those stricken with coronavirus. Whether they recover or die, our task is to help all we can. This practical guide will be the go-to guide for Catholics who want to be equipped to serve others during this crisis."

—Al Kresta
President/CEO, Ave Maria Radio

From the Library of:

Janet Rafferty Gardiner

Sept. 2020
Gift from Billy Smits
Page 81 prayer into photos to send out

Conquering Coronavirus

Teresa Tomeo

conquering Coronavirus

HOW FAITH CAN
PUT YOUR
FEARS TO REST

SOPHIA INSTITUTE PRESS
Manchester, New Hampshire

Sophia Institute Press
Box 5284, Manchester, NH 03108
1-800-888-9344

www.SophiaInstitute.com

Sophia Institute Press® is a registered trademark of Sophia Institute.

paperback ISBN 978-1-64413-326-2
ebook ISBN 978-1-64413-327-9

Library of Congress Control Number: 2020936994

First printing

To my mom, Rosie,
who passed away March 19, 2020,
the feast of St. Joseph,
during the coronavirus pandemic.
Thank you for giving me the gift of life
and the gift of my Catholic Faith.

contents

Introduction. 3

Conquering Coronavirus . . .

    In Our Fearful and Perilous Times 9

    With Small Acts of Generosity 19

    By Caring for the Sick and Feeding the Hungry 27

    By Resurrecting Time-Tested Traditions 35

    Through Complete Spiritual Surrender 51

    By Abandonment to the Will of God 67

    Despite Material and Spiritual Obstacles 73

    Through Brave Community Service 85

    With Faith-Filled Creativity. 93

    By Preaching the Gospel in Words and Deeds 103

    In Your Own Special Circumstances 111

Your Devotional for These Times of Pestilence. 147

Acknowledgments 159

About the Author 161

Conquering Coronavirus

introduction

WHAT COMES TO MIND when you think of the words "conquer" or "conquering"? According to the Merriam-Webster online dictionary, there are quite a few meanings that apply:

- to gain or acquire by force of arms
- to overcome by force of arms: to vanquish
- to gain mastery over or win by overcoming obstacles or opposition
- to overcome by mental or moral power

When we think about conquering a virus—in this case, a pandemic—thoughts related to conquering or overcoming from a medical perspective no doubt pop up almost immediately. We are in a brand-new battle for our health and safety. We're doing our best to support our brave, tireless medical personnel, to practice social distancing, to wash our hands until they're practically raw, and to follow the list of often frustrating restrictions put before us by our government leaders that will hopefully lead to lower numbers of deaths and infections even if not yet to a cure. Certainly, these are all ways to continue to work together, however long it takes, to combat or, God willing, eventually conquer this disease in a very real way and show the coronavirus the proverbial door.

When we turn on the nightly news or check our favorite news websites, in addition to the endless stories, debates, and headlines concerning health, we're bombarded with reports about the virus's frightening economic repercussions. By now, you probably know someone in your circle of family and friends who has lost a job. Perhaps you yourself are going through a painful job loss right now. You may know someone who has died from the virus. Dealing with the loss of a loved one, recovering financially, or conquering a crashing economy: facing any of these tough circumstances takes time.

With these and other challenges in mind, we need more spiritual and moral discussions, insights, and tools to bring about a long-term conquest of this plague. Yes, we've all seen psychologists or counselors weighing in on new and increased tensions within marriages and families due to stay-at-home orders. Concerns have also been raised about increased cases of depression, domestic violence, and even suicide. Christian teachers and advisers have offered plenty of ideas about how to use the extra time we have on our hands. But the coronavirus, although unprecedented in our lifetime, is not the only challenge that has come our way.

This hit me like a ton of bricks as I was covering the pandemic on my daily radio show. We need to stop, take stock, reflect, and zoom out to get a bigger picture of what God might be trying to tell us concerning much more than our immediate needs and circumstances.

Well-known Catholic teacher, radio host, and executive director of Acts XXIX ministry Fr. John Riccardo says this is the time in which God has destined you and me to be alive. In an inspirational video released in early April, Fr. Riccardo explained that he feels God is calling you, me, him, the nation, and the entire world to go much deeper:

> I feel like God is exposing in my own life, in the life of our country, and in our world many of the idols that we have wrongly and falsely put our trust in — reminding us that there is only one source of ultimate lasting hope. There is only one person we can bank on, that we can trust will always be faithful, and that's God.

One of those idols against which we often struggle, myself included, is fear. It helps me to think of the word "fear" as an acronym for "False Evidence Appearing Real." It's easy to fret, to worry, and to work ourselves into a frenzy, thinking that the worst is waiting for us around every corner. That's not to say we should take this pandemic lightly. Just trying to stay informed on its developments can be downright frightening. But we should not let fear control us. In a special message delivered on a rainy evening in Rome from a dark St. Peter's Square, on March 27, 2020, Pope Francis addressed these very real coronavirus-related concerns by quoting from the Gospel of St. Mark, which tells how Jesus calmed the storm on the sea of Galilee. Jesus had fallen asleep in the fishing boat as a ferocious storm moved in. The apostles were stunned. There He was, sleeping the night away, while they were about to sink, or so they believed. The waves that were crashing over the side of their tiny fishing vessel caused them to fear for their lives, even though they had the Creator of the universe sitting right next to them.

The reflection the pope shared was a very important one, and not just because it was the leader of the worldwide Catholic Church speaking. This message, known as *Urbi et orbi* (to the city [of Rome] and the world), is usually reserved for Christmas and Easter. The urgency of the coronavirus changed that. And a homily that normally would be only a blip on the secular media's radar screen, received major attention.

Pope Francis said:

> "When evening had come ..." (Mark 4:35). The Gospel passage we have just heard begins like this. For weeks now it has been evening. Thick darkness has gathered over our squares, our streets, and our cities; it has taken over our lives, filling everything with a deafening silence and a distressing void that stops everything as it passes by; we feel it in the air, we notice it in people's gestures; their glances give them away. We find ourselves afraid and lost. Like the disciples in the Gospel, we were caught off guard by an unexpected, turbulent storm.

The pope goes on to note that regardless of our faith background, we can identify with the apostles: we are all in the middle of some wild, unpredictable weather.

> The storm exposes our vulnerability and uncovers those false and superfluous certainties around which we have constructed our daily schedules, our projects, our habits and priorities. It shows us how we have allowed to become dull and feeble the very things that nourish, sustain, and strengthen our lives and our communities.

We have life-altering choices to make as we continue to navigate our way through the winds and waves brought on by this pandemic. We can choose either to be swallowed up by fear, despair, and negativity or to invite God into — or back into — our lives as never before. This book will help you choose the latter by providing, among other things:

- a collection of stories showing God addressing the crisis through everyday people
- examples of how obstacles can become for you opportunities for stronger relationships with God and others
- reflection questions allowing for group or personal study
- practical guidelines for overcoming fear and for growing in faith
- a variety of resources for prayer and personal reflection
- ideas for further growth and evangelization

Because of the comprehensive media coverage of this continuing crisis, it would take hundreds, possibly thousands, of books to contain all the touching examples of sacrifice along with simple acts of kindness that are being performed across the country and around the globe. I've chosen several of my favorites relating to the different issues we're dealing with as a result of the virus. They're meant to serve you as little pick-me-ups or a ray of sunshine for those times when you start to feel overwhelmed.

So read on and take comfort in the fact that God is not asleep while this storm threatens our lives and our livelihoods — far from it. As a matter of fact, as you'll soon see on the following pages, neither are His people. He is busy working through them. You may recognize yourself, your neighbor, your pastor, or a local police officer in some of the uplifting stories I've collected. Through the chapter on obstacles and opportunities, you might be able to recall an earlier challenge in your own life that led to new beginnings. Resources cited throughout the book may help you find a go-to prayer site or another website where you'll regularly receive comfort and insight.

And as you read on, remember this: we're fooling ourselves, big time, if we believe that curing the coronavirus, finding a new job, replenishing our bank accounts, and being able to step back inside our places of worship or our favorite pubs again will solve all our problems. Problems and challenges we will always have with us. We can truly *conquer* them, along with our fears, only by going deeper in our relationship with God. The more we open our hearts, the more we will recognize how He is revealing Himself in many wonderful, unexpected, and sometimes seemingly simple or small ways. As tough as the situation is right now, this time of suffering could end up being for you the means to a real, long-lasting, positive change. As an old saying goes, "It's not the challenges or difficulties that define us, but rather how we respond to them."

1

CONQUERING CORONAVIRUS

In Our Fearful and Perilous Times

All things work for good for those who love God,
who are called according to his purpose.

—Romans 8:28, NABRE

"THE LENTIEST LENT WE'VE EVER LENTED." Those words make up my favorite meme, which gained great traction on social media during the first few months of 2020. Even those who aren't Catholic or Christian found themselves relating to this catchy phrase, as recently, thanks to the coronavirus, we've all been put through some version of our own "Lentiest Lent." Although Lent is only a six-week religious season beginning on Ash Wednesday and ending right before Easter Sunday, in 2020 it felt as if it would never end.

One day, we were going about our lives: working, studying, praying, playing, and tending to our families. The next day, or so it seemed, we were face-to-face with something that looked and felt like a modern-day horror movie—our own version of the zombie apocalypse. When I see doctors and nurses covered from head to toe in protective gear, it's like watching a live remake of the 1995 film *Outbreak*, starring Dustin Hoffman. Although that movie is twenty-five years old, the story about Hoffman's character, a doctor trying to find a cure for a deadly virus traced to a foreign land, strikes eerily close to home.

But it's not Hollywood that has struck us.

It's real life—real life in the form of a pandemic that's turning everything upside down. As of this writing, the long-term impact of the coronavirus is still hidden. Within just these first few months of the outbreak in the United States, the pandemic has taken tens of thousands of lives and forced the layoffs of millions of workers.

A virus that takes thousands of lives, shuts down the economy, and forces a vast majority of residents to stay behind closed doors, not just for days or weeks but for months: those of us living in sophisticated first-world countries such as the United States of America were certain that such a thing could never happen here. Not in my backyard!

Nonetheless, although it may have begun on the other side of the world, it soon arrived at our borders, moved through our cities, and ended up literally right at our front doors.

COVID-19 is painting a dramatically different daily landscape in many areas of our lives, even erasing simple pleasures such as dinners at our favorite restaurant and leisurely afternoons of shopping at the local mall. Within a New York minute the color-ful scenery was replaced with strokes of darkness and confusion, and images of emptiness and shock as every other activity we took for granted was stripped from our regular routines. Offices, schools, and churches were closed indefinitely. For Catholics, that meant no public Masses, no weddings, funerals, or baptisms. Churches in Rome — including St. Peter's Basilica — closed their doors. The Church of the Holy Sepulchre, built on the site of the tomb of Christ in the Holy Land, was shut down for the first time since the Black Plague, nearly seven hundred years ago. Other major religions did the same, canceling services and all public gatherings.

What was happening? How could this be? When will it be over?

The even larger, more haunting question for so many, including people of faith, and the main reason I wrote this book, remains: Where is God in all of this?

Across faith and lifestyle spectrums, people are searching for inspiration and answers and in a very direct way. According to research released in March of 2020 by the Association for the Study of Religion, Economics, and Culture, the number of Google searches for the word "prayer" greatly increased as the coronavirus continued to make headlines. That research examined Internet searches in seventy-five countries and found that "search intensity for 'prayer' doubles for every 80,000 new registered cases of COVID-19."[1] In March of 2020, the Association discovered that Internet searches for "prayer" reached the highest level in the past five years for which research was available, surpassing all other major events, including Christmas, Easter, and Ramadan.

We're no doubt still in the middle of the crisis. With all of this on our plates, our natural inclination is to reach out for help. We worry. We wonder. We may even believe that because of all the self-centeredness in our society, which long ago left God in the dust, we had it coming—and big time!

Whatever may be pressing on our hearts, God desires us to reach out to Him. He can more than handle the fears and the questions. In this opportune moment, what God is looking for from us, His most precious creation, is an intimate relationship. I don't know about you, but the hunger and the searching occurring right now remind me a lot of what happened after 9-11.

---

[1] Carol Glatz, "Googling 'Prayer' Has Skyrocketed with Coronavirus Spread, Expert Says," *Crux*, April 4, 2020, cruxnow.com/church-in-the-usa/2020/04/googling-prayer-has-skyrocketed-with-coronavirus-spread-expert-says/.

That day and in the weeks thereafter, there was a great surge of interest in matters of faith.

Unfortunately, it was short-lived.

On September 11, 2002 — exactly one year after the terrorist attacks — as part of an online report covering church attendance, Fox News highlighted a very disheartening survey:

> The emotional pain and search for answers after Sept. 11 had many flocking to religious services like never before. A surge of spirituality occurred as Americans examined just how fragile life was and evaluated what was important. Answers were hard to come by in the months that followed the attacks, and many sought solace in a higher power.
>
> But, like many of the initial post-attack phenomena, church attendance has since returned to normal.
>
> "After 9/11 we had 20-some odd thousand people show up," said Senior Pastor Ed Young. "The largest crowd in the history of Fellowship Church.... And when I walked on stage I looked around and said, 'Where have you guys been? It takes something like this for you to show up to church?'"
>
> But the pews were soon roomier.
>
> "I was disappointed somewhat that more didn't stick around. We dropped ... to 16 or 17 thousand the next weekend and then the weekend after that to about 14,500," he said.
>
> By some estimates, on the Sunday following the terror attacks roughly half of the adult population in the United States attended a religious service. But the attendance dropped off starting in November.

The report quoted statistics[2] from the religious-research polling firm Barna that revealed that participation in church-based activities quickly went back to what it was before the attacks.

Forty-two percent of Americans polled said they attended services and 84 percent said they prayed before Sept. 11. And now, 43 percent say they attend services and 83 percent say they pray.

Shortly after the doors of my local church were closed due to the pandemic, I was able to follow our Saturday vigil Mass online and was blessed to hear a poignant homily by Fr. Rich Bartoszek. Fr. Rich not only helps out at the weekend Masses at my parish but also serves as a full-time chaplain for one of the major hospital systems in the Archdiocese of Detroit. By the time he celebrated this particular Mass, he had witnessed firsthand the devastation caused by the coronavirus. As Fr. Rich explained, many folks he bumped into in the busy hospital hallways told him they were fearful. They had a lot of "God-related" questions. Some were even convinced, as some were after 9-11, that this is a judgment or some sort of punishment from God.

Fr. Rich told his co-workers the same thing that he told parishioners tuning in that Saturday: the God we serve is not using the pandemic or any other crisis to zap us. He didn't cause it, but He allows it so we can help reveal Him to the world.

For most of us, we have never seen anything like this. But this is not what our God does. I choose to see exactly what

---

[2] "How America's Faith Has Changed Since 9-11," Barna, November 26, 2001, www.barna.com/research/how-americas-faith-has-changed-since-9-11/.

Jesus says, "that the works of God might be made visible," through what is going on in the world right now.

He framed his message around the Gospel reading for March 22. We know that there are no coincidences, and those verses were a clear reminder that God is right here with us in the coronavirus trenches. In the ninth chapter of John's Gospel, we read about Jesus healing the man who was born blind. Upon seeing the blind man, the disciples ask Jesus to tell them who sinned, the man or his parents. Given the beliefs of that time, they were no doubt surprised by the Lord's response:

> Neither he nor his parents sinned; it is so that the works of God might be made visible through him. (John 9:3, NABRE)

Do we recognize the works of God in the events of our day, or are we still paralyzed by fear? Although we would never have chosen for ourselves this "Lentiest Lent we've ever Lented," it might at the end of the day wind up being one of the most profound periods of our lives, helping us spiritually to conquer not only coronavirus but a whole lot more.

PERSONAL

reflection

In what ways has this been your
"Lentiest Lent ever Lented"?

What spiritual steps are you taking to conquer
your fears that are related to the coronavirus?

How has this pandemic changed
the way you live your faith?

Have you shared about this change
with your friends and family?

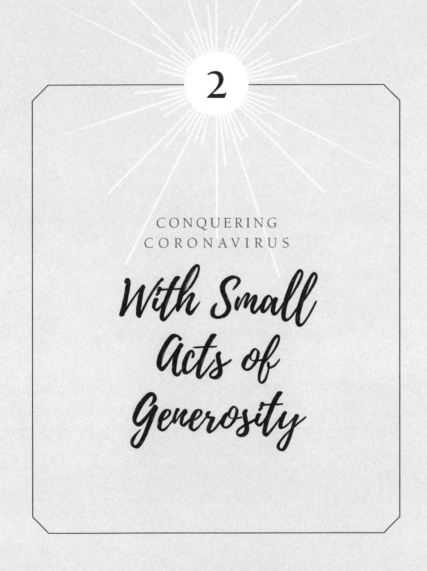

2

CONQUERING
CORONAVIRUS

With Small
Acts of
Generosity

He who is faithful in a very little is faithful also in much.

—Luke 16:10

THIS YEAR, ST. PATRICK'S Day here in southeastern Michigan was exceptionally lovely. I spent the bright, sunny day, however, inside my elderly mother's quaint apartment at her assisted-living facility. After yet another visit to the ER, she had been sent back home and this time placed in hospice care as a result of congestive heart failure, kidney failure, and several other ailments that come from being almost ninety-four years old. The doctors said it would be only a matter of days before she passed away.

It was one of the loneliest and most challenging times of my life.

It's never easy to lose a loved one, but having it happen in the middle of a pandemic causes all kinds of additional anxiety and emotional stress. It felt as if I were being engulfed by a deep fog of grief and confusion. No one knew how this pandemic would work itself out. Even now, none of us know.

Normally, visiting my mom, Rosie, was an absolute delight. The assisted-living center was always decorated beautifully and filled with fun activities. I often joked with her that I enjoyed her place more than she did. At least three afternoons a week, they offered great entertainment in the lobby. There was happy hour every Friday at 3:00 p.m., which you'd better believe I rarely missed. There were prayer groups, Bible studies, and a weekly

Mass for Catholic residents. It was wonderful to see my mother doing what she could in her limited capacity, for the two years she resided there, trying to make the most of it.

By St. Patrick's Day, thanks to COVID-19, all those activities had come to a screeching halt, not just for Mom, but for all the residents. Since many of the virus-related deaths in the United States and Europe were occurring among the elderly, nursing homes and assisted-living centers were among the first locations to go into serious lockdown. Visitors were allowed only for emergency or life-and-death situations. At my mother's location, no one could enter without first having his or her temperature taken and filling out a long health questionnaire. Overnight, the atmosphere went from upbeat to somber.

As I was sitting in my mother's room, listening to her labored breathing, I thought that, if life were normal, the apartment would have been filled with her grandchildren, great-grandchildren, and her many friends, both old and new.

Without them, it felt very strange.

As those thoughts were crossing my mind, I heard a knock at the door. One of the employees told me to go to the large picture window. Outside, there was a surprise waiting.

Although my mother remained sound asleep, I described to her what was happening. Right outside her window, there was a very cheerful woman with two very large dogs. The dogs were decked out in St. Patrick's Day garb: shamrocks, shimmery bright green tutus, and other bling. Apparently, as I later learned, the dog owner lived in the neighborhood and was very concerned about the residents feeling alone and isolated—especially on a day when there normally would be a lot of celebrating. So she dressed up her pups and took her time doing window visits to each of the apartments. Keep in mind that although this is only a one-story facility, there are dozens of apartments: probably close to seventy residents. As you can imagine, her visits probably took her all afternoon and then some. I was so moved that I went outside to thank her and the employees making the rounds with her. If it impacted me, imagine the impact it had on the elderly stuck inside.

My mother died two days later, on the feast of St. Joseph. The St. Patrick's Day scene outside her window was cemented in my mind and kept me going as we began to pack her things and prepare for her funeral.

Yes, the actions of the St. Pat's visitor might pale in comparison with the amazing feats of the tireless medical personnel, EMS workers, and others on the frontlines who continue to fight this invisible enemy while often putting their own health and safety in harm's way. But I share this story with you because I'm quite certain, knowing the media as well as I do, that her actions would not be deemed newsworthy enough to make the rounds on the talks shows, Twitter, or Facebook. It might have been a small deed, but for me it was a big deal. God was providing me with some badly needed blue skies on a dreary day, reminding me that I was not alone.

When we look at all the bills that pile up on our desks each month, eliminating just one of them might be considered a nice little break, but no big deal in the overall financial scheme of things—unless, thanks to the economic fallout of the coronavirus, you're among the millions of Americans who have lost their jobs or are among those having a tough time in general making ends meet. That's why Brooklyn Catholic landlord Mario Salerno decided to waive the April rent for all—yes, all—of his two hundred tenants. He did not divulge to the Catholic media outlet EWTN News just how much the gracious "little" gift cost him. He did share that his Catholic faith led to his decision.

And I'm guessing that the mini concerts given by Italian opera singer Maurizio Marchini from his balcony were a big hit for residents of Florence, Italy. On March 11, sixty million people across Italy went on quarantine in their homes. The beautiful streets of this Renaissance city were deserted, as were the streets in the rest of the nation. This famous vocalist didn't do just one impromptu concert, but several. The original video of Marchini belting out the popular Puccini aria "Nessun Dorma" from *Turandot* went viral and prompted other balcony concerts of all shapes, sizes, and sounds throughout the country.

The United Kingdom's newspaper the *Guardian* reported a huge response to a social media invitation calling for anyone who played an instrument to go to his or her balcony or window to perform. More videos of Italian citizens in lockdown continued to circulate on social media. One recording that was made in the stunning Tuscan hill town of Siena, the *Guardian* reports, has been viewed well over six hundred thousand times. The clip shows several residents singing a traditional song from their windows. A few days after all the music began, the Italians chose a Saturday afternoon to honor the medical community by opening the shutters, leaning out of their windows, and offering a nationwide round of applause.

They applauded, sang, danced, and played their favorite instruments to boost the morale of their fellow Italians. They exhibited, as did my mother's sweet St. Patrick's Day visitor, that no gift of one's time and talent is too small when it comes to conquering sadness and fear. Their actions also prove that although coronavirus is extremely contagious, so is kindness.

PERSONAL

reflection

Describe a small act of kindness that has
made a difference in your life recently
as it relates to the pandemic.

Ask your family to talk about their
favorite stories of people helping
people during this pandemic.

In what little ways are you sharing
Christ's love with those in need?

3

CONQUERING
CORONAVIRUS

By Caring for the Sick and Feeding the Hungry

Whether you eat or drink, whatever you do, do it all for the glory of God.

—1 Corinthians 10:31

THE GLORY OF GOD is probably the last thing that comes to mind when you see the awful stories on the news showing folks fighting over the last carton of milk, a loaf of bread, and, oh yes, those last precious rolls of toilet paper on the supermarket shelves.

Let's be honest.

By now, we all know far too well that the coronavirus is an illness that will be with us for years to come. But the fearmongering by a good portion of the media has led to panic buying, hoarding, and hysteria. People were convinced that stores would run out of every morsel, even though there is practically a grocery or big-box store on every corner in every town of the good ol' USA. Those embarrassing scenes that were running on a perpetual loop on some networks haven't been among our proudest moments, to say the least.

Call me an eternal optimist, but I think we can erase the ugliness of those food fights and replace them with examples of real food for serious thought and reflection. All we need to do is remember that the good news stories, when it comes to people stepping up to the plate, so to speak, far outweigh the bad, despite what CNN and the *New York Times* may want you to believe.

Grab your memory remote and click over to the JOY channel, as in "Jesus first, Others second, Yourself last." Meet seven-year-old

Cavanaugh Bell, who started his own online campaign to help elderly folks in his Maryland neighborhood impacted by the virus. In addition to the dollars raised, he also donated $500 of his own cash to the cause. Think about all the other things a little boy might want to do with his birthday and Christmas money. He could easily have purchased a new bike, video games, or a new computer. Instead he headed to the store and did the shopping for someone other than himself, purchasing frozen food, fresh fruits, sanitary wipes, and other grocery items in order to put together some sixty-five care packages. He took them to a senior community in his neighborhood.

Officer Danny Christiansen from West Valley City, Utah, did a fine job of representing law enforcement and Americans in general when he helped a Vietnamese restaurant in his area. A hundred dollars' worth of food may not seem like a major cost to some, but if you were suddenly forced to keep the doors of your establishment open only by way of carry-out orders, you probably wouldn't see it as chump change. Christiansen stopped by the restaurant after learning of an apparent prank. Someone had ordered one hundred dollars' worth of sushi but never showed up to pay for it. Christiansen bought the sushi and shared it with his fellow police officers, prompting the restaurant owner to say that his thoughtfulness restored her faith in people.

Then there is the major Metro Detroit grocery distributor, Value Wholesale Distributors, that turned its large, very successful family-owned delivery business into a face-shield factory practically overnight. They got together with another local company and began cranking out more than two thousand shields daily. The badly needed face shields are being distributed to health-care professionals on the frontlines who are fighting the virus. If you spoke to the owners, brothers Matthew and Brian Loussia, they would tell you that this is what they do: they take care of family, and now, thanks to the pandemic, their grocery business is "feeding" a much larger clan in a different way.

And weren't my husband and I pleasantly surprised when we opened our door one Saturday morning to find a bag of delicious bagels on our front porch! There was no card or note—only a menu from the local deli down the street. At first, I thought there was a mistake with the delivery of the order, so I gave them a call. No mistake at all. They just wanted to make us aware that they were thinking of the people in the neighborhood and would remain open for carry-out orders. This deli is a small business. It would have been thoughtful enough for one of their employees to drop off menus and leave it at that. Our street alone is at least a half mile long, and according to the pleasant person on the other end of the phone, the employees of the deli had randomly delivered bagels to four or five streets in our area.

In my home state of Michigan, a survey by the Restaurant and Lodging Association showed that the coronavirus pandemic is hitting restaurants very hard. Association president Justin Winslow says at least 72,000 jobs were lost in the first three months of 2020, along with 491 million dollars in sales. Many restaurants are indicating that they'll soon be closed forever.

Take another glance at those stats, and think about the generosity of that little bagel shop. It doesn't take a math whiz to figure out that those bags of bagels represent, in more ways than one, an awful lot of dough.

Feeding the hungry is one of the Corporal Works of Mercy, found in the teachings of Jesus:

> I was hungry and you gave me food, I was thirsty and you
> gave me drink, I was a stranger and you welcomed me, I

was naked and you clothed me, I was sick and you visited me, I was in prison and you came to me. (Matt. 25:35–36)

The Corporal Works of Mercy concern the physical and material needs of others. According to the United States Conference of Catholic Bishops (USCCB), they give us the model for how we are to treat our fellow man: "They respond to the basic needs of humanity as we journey together through this life."

And what a journey this is! As we continue to make our way along this new, often treacherous and bumpy path carved out by the pandemic, let's slow down a bit and take stock of what we're carrying and what we're willing to share. Hopefully we're following the lead of Officer Christiansen or Cavanaugh Bell and packing plenty of nourishment for both body and soul.

PERSONAL
reflection

———————

How has the pandemic made you more
aware of the basic needs of others?

How are you practicing the Corporal
Works of Mercy in your family?

What types of faith activities help
"feed" you and your loved ones?

4

By Resurrecting Time-Tested Traditions

*Return to the LORD, your God, for he is gracious and
merciful, slow to anger, and abounding in steadfast love.*

—Joel 2:13

WHETHER OR NOT YOU have children at home, I think you'll appreciate another clever meme making the rounds on social media platforms. A good friend of mine who is a retired teacher shared it with me shortly after the lockdowns around the country and the world began:

I'm expelling my children from homeschool.

No matter how tight you are as a family, every family comes with its own set of issues. And oh, how those issues can be exacerbated when we're together 24/7 for weeks or months on end! The sometimes too-close-for-comfort arrangements have prompted many of us, out of frustration or sheer exhaustion, to ask, "Is this really our new normal?"

Or, in the words of the psalmist King David, "How long, O LORD?" (Ps. 13:1).

At the time I'm writing this book, stay-at-home mandates have been extended, along with public school closures in too many districts to list here. We still don't have clear answers to the above questions. In the meantime, let me propose that instead of giving in to the desire to expel or send packing your kids, spouse, or anyone else under your roof, even if it's only to the backyard, you might benefit greatly from looking at this situation differently. Instead of a new normal, think about the benefits of the "old" normal.

This was suggested by the associate pastor at my church, Fr. John Bettin, who made the "old normal" the focus of a very powerful Lenten homily.

> This phrase "the new normal": I submit to you today that it is not a new norm; it's the old norm revisited. It's the old norm 2.0. It's the old norm when we gathered at dinner and prayed together and prayed the blessing before meals. We were together as a family. We ate together on Sunday, even getting on each other's nerves until Dad said, "Be quiet again and finish your meal." That was family life. Everyone helped one another. We looked out for our neighbors. We shoveled the snow. We mowed the lawn for our neighbors without being asked, and yes, that old cliché, we helped the old lady across the street. People actually did those things, and then something happened over time where we became centered and focused on ourselves—not everybody, but society in general.

As mentioned previously, for a brief period after the terrorist attacks of 9-11, we made real efforts to reprioritize and get closer to God and family. The seemingly never-ending funerals of fire fighters, police officers, and civilians killed in New York, Washington, D.C., and Pennsylvania pulled us together and prompted all of us to hug our spouses, parents, children, and friends more frequently. We realized how blessed we were as a nation. We filled the pews. Republicans and Democrats gathered in the Big Apple to belt out their own version of "New York, New York." The love and camaraderie were nice while they lasted, but unfortunately, they didn't last very long. Soon enough, we allowed the ways of the busy, hectic world to move in. In some ways we suffered a major case of inflated ego, with "ego" being an acronym to remind us that we "eased God out." Some of us grew comfortable again, once the source of the threats was identified, and the country began to rebuild. Many active Catholics and even some of their leaders did not respond appropriately and practically to the new persons who were suddenly showing up on Sundays.

The founder of Catholic Missionary Disciples, Marcel LeJeune, says that while we certainly welcomed people into our churches in 2001, there wasn't a system in place in our parishes to do the follow-up necessary to help them grow. In a discussion on *Catholic Connection* on April 7 regarding evangelization, LeJeune said this could be one of the reasons God is allowing us to go through this cross:

> We have to look at the culture we have created in the Catholic Church. I would say we have not been all that good at community in our parishes in a wide measure. I think that what ended up happening was that a lot of those folks after 9-11 were going to church, going to Mass again, but they were doing so anonymously. And they had no one to walk with them, no one to evangelize them. Really, they needed people, more mature Christians, to be in their life, to help them out. And they didn't have that and so it was easy to walk away. And I think this might be an opportunity for you and me and for others to say: Okay, how is it that we as a Church need to mature, and what is it that God wants of the parishes? You see there is innovation in social relations that is happening right now that hasn't happened in generations. Maybe it wasn't happening decades ago, but it is now because of the crisis.

So, can we use this as an opportunity that God has put before us to be more innovative, more experimental? Let's work on the weak parts. I really believe this is a moment of grace.

Fast-forward almost twenty years from 9-11. An October 2019 religious landscape study[3] by the Pew Research Center found that Christianity continued to decline at a rapid pace, while the number of Americans with no religious affiliation, those so-called nones, are on the rise:

> Both Protestantism and Catholicism are experiencing losses of population share. Currently, 43% of U.S. adults identify with Protestantism, down from 51% in 2009. And one-in-five adults (20%) are Catholic, down from 23% in 2009. Meanwhile, all subsets of the religiously unaffiliated population—a group also known as religious "nones"—have seen their numbers swell. Self-described atheists now account for 4% of U.S. adults, up modestly but significantly from 2% in 2009; agnostics make up 5% of U.S. adults, up from 3% a decade ago; and 17% of Americans now describe their religion as "nothing in particular," up from 12% in 2009. Members of non-Christian religions also have grown modestly as a share of the adult population.

This followed an even more alarming Pew Research survey concerning core Catholic beliefs that came out in August 2019.

---

[3] "In U.S., Decline of Christianity Continues at Rapid Pace," Pew Research Center, October 17, 2019, www.pewforum. org/2019/10/17/in-u-s-decline-of-christianity-continues-at-rapid-pace/.

According to Pew, just one-third of Catholics agreed with their Church that the Eucharist is the Body and Blood of Christ.[4]

> Transubstantiation—the idea that during Mass, the bread and wine used for Communion become the body and blood of Jesus Christ—is central to the Catholic faith. Indeed, the Catholic Church teaches that the Eucharist is the source and summit of the Christian life. But a new Pew Research Center survey finds that most self-described Catholics don't believe this core teaching. In fact, nearly seven-in-ten Catholics (69%) say they personally believe that during Catholic Mass, the bread and wine used in Communion "are symbols of the body and blood of Jesus Christ." Just one-third of U.S. Catholics (31%) say they believe that "during Catholic Mass, the bread and wine actually become the body and blood of Jesus."

What happened? After such a major wake-up call in 2001, how could we drift so far away God, and what can we do to embrace, as Fr. John Bettin says, an "old" normal? Part of the reaction is our fallen human nature. We cry out to God, just as the Israelites did repeatedly in the Old Testament when times got tough. Then, when they were safe and comfortable again, they not only drifted away from their faith but also replaced God with pagan idols, including that infamous golden calf.

Sound familiar?

---

[4] Gregory A. Smith, "Just One-Third of U.S. Catholics Agree with Their Church That Eucharist Is Body, Blood of Christ," Pew Research Center, August 5, 2019, www.pewresearch. org/fact-tank/2019/08/05/transubstantiation-eucharist-u-s-catholics/.

How ironic—or prophetic, is it?—that the word "corona" in Latin and Italian means "crown"? The World Health Organization declared the virus a pandemic on March 11, 2020, two weeks into the Lenten season.

God didn't cause this virus, but He did allow it to happen at a time when Christians are called to return to Him, to recognize the idols or crowns that we've allowed to take His place. Those idols could be drugs or pornography or an excessive attachment to money or sports. Or they could be an attachment to something just as pervasive, such as too much screen time.

Some of the most recent statistics, including an alarming 2018 study[5] from Nielsen, show Americans now spend most of their waking hours—eleven to twelve hours on average—listening to music, watching TV, using apps on their smartphones, or otherwise consuming media.

Americans are hardly the exception when it comes to spending too much time with technology. In a March 18, 2020, interview[6] with the Italian newspaper *La Repubblica*, Pope Francis offered some advice for families on how to handle the challenges presented by COVID-19:

Some families eat together at home in silence—not because they are listening to one another but because the

[5] Ashley Rodriguez, "Americans Are Now Spending 11 Hours Each Day Consuming Media," Quartz, July 31, 2018, qz.com/1344501/americans-now-spend-11-hours-with-media-in-an-average-day-study/.

[6] "Pope Francis on Facing Challenges of the Coronavirus Pandemic," Vatican News, March 18, 2020, www.vaticannews.va/en/pope/news/2020-03/pope-coronavirus-interview-repubblica-pandemic-covid-coronavirus.html.

parents are watching television while they eat, or their children are on their mobile phones.

The pope went so far as to say that some Italian families could be described as monks, and not in a good or prayerful way. Instead, he said, they're isolated from one another:

> There is no communication here. But listening to one another is important because we understand one another's needs, struggles, and desires.

The concern over media influence on the family has been a reoccurring theme for the pope. During his December 29, 2019, Angelus address, the message given in St. Peter's Square every Sunday, Pope Francis encouraged families to put away their cell phones at mealtimes. The day of that address just happened to be the feast of the Holy Family, a liturgical celebration in the Catholic Church set aside to honor Jesus, His mother Mary, and Joseph, Jesus' earthly father:

> We have to get back to communicating in our families. Fathers, parents, children, grandparents, brothers and sisters, this is a task to undertake today, on the day of the Holy Family. They prayed, worked, and communicated with each other. I ask myself if your family knows how to communicate, or are you like those kids at meal tables where everyone is chatting on their mobile phones, where there is silence like at a Mass?

Then, at the start of Lent 2020, the pope told us yet one more time to put down the phones and turn off the televisions. We live in a world, he said, polluted by "too much verbal violence," which often includes offensive, harmful words. His advice was to put down the phone and pick up the Bible, spending more time as families in prayer, talking to God.

> Lent is a time to disconnect from the cell phones and connect to the Gospel. It is time to give up useless words, chatter, and talk, and speak directly to the Lord. Fasting is not only losing weight; it is also seeking the beauty of a simple life.

The pope sounds a lot like Fr. John Bettin, one of his younger shepherds. Both are calling for a return to what used to be commonplace or that "old" normal. Additional research backs them up further in terms of the importance of family mealtime, not meals where we just happen to be eating at the same table with others.

A 2016 study[7] by the Dallas research firm Toluna revealed that 47 percent—nearly half—of those surveyed said that they share fewer meals with their families, compared with when they were growing up. And a whopping 57 percent admitted that when they do eat together, they're often distracted by technology.

The Center on Addiction released an eye-opening survey[8] in 2012 that connected tech-free family meals to lower instances of substance abuse among teens.

> Our surveys have consistently found a relationship between children having frequent dinners with their parents and a decreased risk of their smoking, drinking, or

---

[7] "Study Shows Trends in Family Mealtimes," Refrigerated and Frozen Foods, May 26, 2016, www.refrigeratedfrozenfood.com/articles/90952-study-shows-trends-in-family-mealtimes.

[8] "The Importance of Family Dinners VIII," Center on Addiction, September 2012, www.centeronaddiction.org/addiction-research/reports/importance-of-family-dinners-2012.

using other drugs, and that parental engagement fostered around the dinner table is one of the most potent tools to help parents raise healthy, drug-free children. Simply put, frequent family dinners make a big difference.

Notice that the Center on Addiction said parental engagement, not engagement with technology. I'm not suggesting tossing out all the computers, televisions, smartphones, and other devices. Right now, technology, when it's correctly utilized, is a huge gift. During a time of isolation, it keeps us connected to friends and extended family. It can also keep us connected to our Faith in a variety of helpful and instructional ways. But how many more studies do we need; how many additional pleas from our Church leaders must we hear before we take seriously their calls for more balance?

There's no time like the present to make some healthy changes, especially since more time at home with each other is, despite the fact that our loved ones get on our nerves at times, one of the silver linings of this huge, dark, pandemic cloud hanging over our heads. Here are a few simple steps to take to help you and your family return to and profit from that "old" normal:

- *Attend virtual church services together as a family.* Even though, as I write this, attending church or Mass in person is still not possible, families can still attend church and "go to Mass" just as they used to do every weekend. There are so many opportunities to "attend" online through livestreaming that you could make choosing the outlet each week a family activity. Protestant services, too, can be found almost everywhere online.
- *Keep mealtimes media-free.* And this goes for parents and children.

- *Take turns saying grace before meals.* This encourages more family engagement and an increased focus on God.
- *Encourage and schedule daily family prayer time.* Have the family choose different days to pray for the many heroes fighting the virus on the frontlines. It could be doctors, nurses, EMS workers, or those caring for elderly shut-ins.
- *Keep computers, TVs, and yes, even cell phones out of bedrooms.* This goes for parents and children. This aids in media accountability efforts, ensures healthier sleeping habits, and avoids excessive media usage.
- *Engage the media as a family.* Choosing family-friendly programs or movies to enjoy together can foster closeness as well as help parents set good examples concerning wise media choices.
- *Vow as a family to make the changes permanent.* Hopefully sooner rather than later, the coronavirus will be a thing of the past, but our good new "old" habits need to stay with us. Encourage one another to continue in them. Life will no doubt get in the way of them from time to time, but do your best to stick with those new habits. My husband and I came back to the Church through a Bible study group, so we try our best to do the daily Mass readings every morning. That practice continues to this day, twenty-seven years and counting.

There was something else that Fr. Bettin said in his homily that stuck with me. He referred to the coronavirus as "God's calling card," a real invitation from God asking us to turn back to Him and to our Faith, to rediscover that old norm. God did not bring about or cause this virus. But He did allow it to happen in order for us to learn, to grow, and to reevaluate the way we live our lives. In this sense, it is God's loving invitation to grow closer to Him and to others.

This Lent you will remember for the rest of your lives—that God is calling us back to Himself. I think the coronavirus is God's calling card. We have this great opportunity to turn back to God. Too many times we turn our backs on Him and look to the world for solutions to our problems—look to the world for that crutch to get us through life. COVID-19 is His calling card to us, that we return to Him and turn to one another, loving God and one another. And what a great opportunity! My hope is that we continue to do so beyond when a cure is found, beyond when there is no more fear. Let us hearken back and remember these days.

PERSONAL
reflection

What steps can you take to help you and
your family return to the old normal?

Conduct a media reality check in your family
by making an honest assessment of how
much and what type of media you consume.

What type of changes do you think
need to be made? Engage your family in
developing and applying the changes.

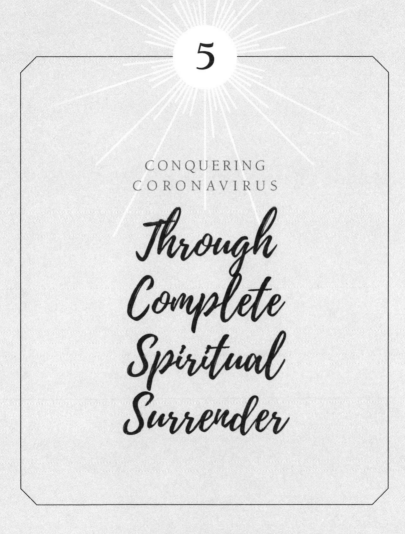

5

CONQUERING
CORONAVIRUS

*Through
Complete
Spiritual
Surrender*

I am the handmaid of the Lord. May it be
done to me according to your word.

—Luke 1:38, NABRE

THE MORNING OF MY mother's burial, surrendering was the last thing on my mind. To be quite blunt, I was in the middle of a major tug-of-war with God. Given the loss, the suffering, and the range of emotions, I thought I had done my share of surrendering at least for a while. It's difficult enough to lose a loved one. Experiencing a death in the family at a time when the entire world is fighting a major pandemic adds layer upon layer of confusion, sadness, fear, and longing.

Let's start with the confusion. For me as a broadcast journalist, the virus is akin to a never-ending breaking story. It is forever changing from one hour to the next. The day my mom passed away, the Catholic Church in the Archdiocese of Detroit was still allowing funeral Masses. Only immediate family members could attend, but some parishes, including mine, did offer the option of livestreaming the Mass from parish websites. That sounded very reasonable to me, and, given that most of my mother's family resided on the East Coast and were too old to travel, the livestreaming option was a blessing.

Plans for the funeral Mass went forward. We were thrilled that our wonderful pastor, Msgr. Bugarin, was able to serve as the celebrant. That's exactly what my mom had requested. Msgr. Bugarin had celebrated my father's funeral Mass ten years earlier, and since both of my parents were very involved in the parish, celebrating the Mass meant a great deal to Msgr. Bugarin as well.

It was on the calendar for Wednesday, March 25. In the Catholic Church, March 25 is the feast of the Annunciation, recognizing the angel Gabriel's announcing to Mary that she was chosen to be the Mother of God. It also happened to be my father's birthday. I kept thinking what a great birthday present this was for my dad and was sure he would be smiling down on us. This might not be everything we hoped for, but it would still be special.

Then, as quickly as I had selected the Scripture readings, prayer cards, and flower arrangements, the rules changed. Michigan and the Detroit area were becoming hot spots for the spread of the coronavirus. All funeral Masses, in addition to all other public Masses, were canceled. All that was left for Catholics was the graveside Rite of Committal. And this is where the sadness, longing, and fear come in. The blessed way our Catholic Faith recognizes the dignity of the human person from conception until natural death is seen in all its glory in the funeral liturgy, as explained by the USCCB:

> At the funeral liturgy, the Church gathers with the family and friends of the deceased to give praise and thanks to God for Christ's victory over sin and death, to commend the deceased to God's tender mercy and compassion, and to seek strength in the proclamation of the Paschal Mystery. The funeral liturgy, therefore, is an act of worship, and not merely an expression of grief.[9]

---

[9]   "An Overview of Catholic Funeral Rites," United States Conference of Catholic Bishops, http://www.usccb.org/prayer-and-worship/bereavement-and-funerals/overview-of-catholic-funeral-rites.cfm.

That beautiful act of worship was not available, at least not yet. I felt cheated. It was sad for me and my family, and the longing for all the beautiful traditions of our Catholic Faith was so strong that I had a hard time getting any rest. Of course, I knew we could and would have a memorial Mass in the future, when the coronavirus coast was clear. But who knew when that would be? I was truly fearful that not many would be able attend once they returned to their busy lives. I was fearful that Mom wouldn't get the incredible send-off that my father did and that I would be judged negatively for somehow not doing enough. Were we doing right by her? Maybe there was some loophole I could find somewhere.

When I woke up the morning of her burial, my tug-of-war with God continued. The weather didn't help matters. The forecasters had predicted partly cloudy to cloudy skies. Surprise, surprise: they were wrong! It was pouring outside. Listening to the rain pounding on our roof, I let my fear take over. Among other crazy things, I envisioned the coffin sliding into the street. I thought for certain the burial might even be canceled, thanks to the weather. My one-sided conversation with God went something like this:

Seriously, Lord? You've got to be kidding me. We can't have a wake, or a Mass? We couldn't even bury Mom on Daddy's birthday? Didn't she deserve at least that much? All we're left with now is a simple graveside service, and how, pray tell, is that going to happen with all this rain? I know You didn't cause the pandemic, but I also know that You calm the storms. I could use a little help here.

I jumped out of bed and rushed downstairs to make coffee. I decided to pick up my Catholic devotional in hopes that the daily Mass readings would change my mood and give me some badly needed spiritual boost. But I got nothin'. I'm sure my Miss Grumpy Pants mood didn't help the situation, but I wasn't interested at that point in surrendering to what was inevitable. I got ready and headed to the funeral home for the private viewing.

I kept thinking as I looked around how different it had been ten years earlier, when my father passed away. His wake had been held in a room just down the hall. It had been so crowded that dozens of additional chairs had to be added to accommodate everyone. My aunts and uncles told stories about growing up with my dad in their strong Italian American family. It was heartwarming to see so much love and support. The celebration of my father's life continued the following day at the funeral Mass.

Not for Mom today!

After some quiet time with a handful of family members, we headed to the cemetery. There we were greeted by yet another set of new coronavirus rules. We were told to remain in our cars while the casket was lowered into the ground. After the workers were done, they would leave, and we could proceed to the graveside for the committal, all the while practicing social distancing, of course.

As I was watching them lower my mother into her grave, I felt so alone. Then unexpectedly, I heard from two of my closest friends. Kelly had already texted me several times, reminding me that she was covering me with prayer, as had my dear friend Gail. What I didn't realize until I spoke with both of them was that, through messages, they had been trying to tell me all morning that my mother was being buried on the birthday of my patron and all-time favorite Catholic saint, Teresa of Avila. When they told me, I burst into tears. For me, this was no small thing. Over the years, including the more than two decades I was away from my Catholic Faith, I still felt a close connection to this saint after whom I was named. She won me over with her own quite bold conversations with God.

Teresa is considered — and not just by Catholics and other Christians — to be a powerful teacher concerning deep spirituality, including the contemplative life, mental prayer, and unique conversations with God. She was a religious reformer, a writer, and a theologian who viewed prayer as "nothing more than being on terms of friendship with God."

While all that makes for a very impressive CV, it was her feisty personality that drew me in. She had absolutely no qualms about telling Jesus exactly how she felt. One of the most famous stories about her directness centers on a long, arduous journey she was making across the rugged Spanish countryside to visit another convent. Her carriage became stuck in the mud, and it turned over, dumping her and her belongings onto the messy hillside. Completely frustrated and discouraged, she looked up to Heaven and cried out, "Lord, if this is the way You treat Your friends, no wonder You have so few!"

Most of us — and I put myself at the very top of this list — may not ever come anywhere remotely close to St. Teresa's holiness. However, we easily relate to her feelings of frustration and abandonment. As much as I love St. Teresa, in all honesty she was not on my mind the day of my mother's burial. That reminder from my friends was the *Godly* coincidence (or another "God-cidence") that I needed to get me through the rest of that very rough morning. That and the fact that the rain suddenly stopped as we were about to begin the service. Thank You, Jesus.

Another close friend of mine, Mary, who walked beside me as my mother was dying, said that a wise priest told her that God doesn't mind one bit when we pound on His chest. And the pounding or whining is, on a very spiritual level, a form of surrender as it begins with at least a recognition that someone other than me, myself, and I is in charge. As Shakespeare's character Hamlet proclaimed, "Aye, there's the rub." Too many of us think we're in control. And when we're blindsided six ways to Sunday by something that our world has never seen the likes of, "there's the rub," that deep-down, annoying feeling that we don't want to acknowledge. If the coronavirus hasn't quite yet awakened in you that voice, also known as conscience, here's a news flash for you: God is the one who's large and in charge. Not us.

Even if you're not dealing with something as drastic as a death in the family during this pandemic, you're no doubt having to do an awful lot of surrendering. As Pope Francis reminded us in his message from St. Peter's Square, we've all been caught off guard by "an unexpected, turbulent storm":

> We have realized that we are on the same boat, all of us fragile and disoriented, but at the same time important and needed, all of us called to row together, each of us in need of comforting the other. On this boat ... are all of us. Just like those disciples, who spoke anxiously with one voice, saying, "We are perishing," so we too have realized that we cannot go on thinking of ourselves, but only together can we do this.

For faithful members of the Catholic Church, among the most difficult aspects of letting go and letting God is being separated from the sacraments, especially from the Eucharist, or Holy Communion. My home archdiocese, the Archdiocese of Detroit, was one of the first to cancel public Masses and funerals. (The sacraments of Confession, or Reconciliation, and the Anointing of the Sick, also known as Last Rites, would still be available.)

When I first heard the announcement, I thought it was over the top. It seemed so counterproductive. At a time when we needed Jesus, Body, Blood, Soul, and Divinity (as our Church teaches), more than ever, how is keeping us from receiving Him the right decision?

The evangelization director of our archdiocese was gracious enough to take live calls on my radio program from other concerned Catholics asking the same question. Within days of the interview, practically every Catholic community across the country and the planet had made the same decision. Soon more details emerged concerning the virus's ability to spread rapidly. Given the physical contact involved with receiving Communion, not to mention the proximity of congregants during Mass and other church services, the move made a lot more sense.

After the painful decision was announced, our archbishop, Allen Vigneron, released "10 Guideposts for Christians in the Time of the Coronavirus Pandemic." Guideposts were a central part of his 2017 pastoral letter, *Unleash the Gospel*, and Archbishop Vigneron stated that he hoped this newest list might provide direction and encouragement, as Christians in southeastern Michigan were dealing with the pandemic-based challenges. In these guideposts, Archbishop Vigneron speaks of this as a time of trial in which we are called to be more Christlike. Specifically, in his second guidepost, the archbishop reminds us that for whatever reason, in 2020, this is the Lent God wanted us to have:

> God in Christ is the Lord of history. He's in charge. His providential plan for our salvation and happiness cannot be defeated. If he has permitted us to have to be for a while without our public celebration of the Holy Eucharist and our usual Lenten devotions, his Spirit offers us

other means to prepare ourselves for Holy Week and the Paschal Triduum.

He also addressed, in his fifth guidepost, the questions being raised about the necessity for the suspension of public Masses, by pointing to the collaboration between holiness and science.

We must resist any idea that there's some sort of divorce between our cooperating with public health officials to mitigate the spread of the virus and our complete trust in God's power to protect us. This guidepost is a variation on the axiom that "nature builds on grace." Our whole-hearted cooperation with the civil authorities involves acts of Christian virtue: acts of justice in doing our part to protect the common good and acts of charity because our motive is love for God and neighbor.

We Catholics are being reintroduced to Spiritual Communion. While following Mass online, or at any time, we're encouraged to say a special prayer recognizing that although we can't receive Jesus physically, we can still receive Him in our hearts:

Spiritual Communion Prayer
*My Jesus, I believe that You are present
in the Most Holy Sacrament.
I love You above all things,
and I desire to receive You into my soul.
Since I cannot at this moment receive You sacramentally,
come at least spiritually into my heart.
I embrace You as if You were already there
and unite myself wholly to You.
Never permit me to be separated from You. Amen.*

I'm hardly a theologian, but it has occurred to me that perhaps God is allowing this to happen so we can deepen our appreciation for Him in the Eucharist. Think back to the statistics released by the Pew Research Center. The 2019 report *What Americans Know about Religion* showed that only one-third of Catholics believe that the Eucharist is the actual Body and Blood of Jesus.

For those of us who have wholeheartedly accepted this core teaching of our Faith, the separation is painful. Part of my continued prayer during this pandemic involves asking God to increase my love and appreciation of this sacrament. How many times have I taken this tremendous gift for granted? How long did I wait to dive more deeply into Church teaching and Scripture to truly understand the basis for this belief? How can I be a witness and better accept this cross in hopes of sharing this teaching with others?

In his book *Journey toward Easter*,[10] published in 1983, Cardinal Ratzinger (Pope Emeritus Benedict XVI) said that this type of spiritual hunger is sometimes necessary:

> Sometimes we need to experience hunger, corporal and spiritual, to appreciate once again the Lord's gifts and to understand the sufferings of our brothers and sisters who are hungry. Bodily and spiritual fasting is a vehicle of love.

So how do we go about surrendering or offering up this cross and other crosses we're carrying right now? Here a few of the steps I've taken to help me in this continual process:

- *Put God first.* Or as I like to say, if God is your copilot, change seats. Commit or recommit your life to Christ

[10] Cardinal Joseph Ratzinger, *Journey toward Easter: Spiritual Reflections for the Lenten Season* (New York: Crossroads, 2006).

by inviting Him to be Lord of your entire life. This means taking your Faith seriously.

- *Make a verbal commitment daily.* Years ago, I got into the habit of trying to say first thing each morning, "Here I am, Lord. I have come to do Your will." It's short, sweet, and to the point. It helps me prioritize and remember that God is flying this plane, not me.

- *Think of the word "Bible" as an acronym for "Basic Instructions before Leaving Earth."* We're doing much better, but Catholics in general are still woefully lacking in a basic knowledge of Scripture, as seen in the Pew Research report. The basis for the Church teaching on the Eucharist appears in a long list of Scripture verses in both the Old and New Testaments. If more Catholics were to read the Bible, those shocking numbers in the Pew survey would be much different. Given the countless resources we have at our fingertips, there is no reason we shouldn't be reading Scripture every day. As Catholics, it's quite easy to be connected to the universal Catholic Church, since the daily Mass readings are the same throughout the world. We can't expect to hear from God if we don't know Him or communicate with Him. The Bible is God's love letter to us.

- *Do not give in to fear.* One of the most frequent statements made by Jesus in Scripture is "Be not afraid." That's easier said than done at times, no doubt. But controlling our fear, rather than allowing it to control us, is what matters. When we're overcome by fear, we make bad decisions. We lose hope and can easily drift away from God. If you need any reminders of this, just go back to some of the stories involving panic-buying, hoarding, and other bad examples of how folks have recently let fear convince them that the sky is falling.

- *Keep a Godwinks or Godcidence journal.* Jot down times when you recognized God working in your life. It could be an answered prayer. It might be that call or text from a friend (like the ones I received on the day of my mom's burial) that comes through right when you need it most. We've all had those incidents that were too uncanny to be mere coincidences. We have short memories, so write them down and refer to them often, reminding yourself just how much you are loved by God.

Surrender doesn't mean throwing to the wind all caution and all the valid concerns we have about the coronavirus. God has given us an intellect. He doesn't drop down massive signs brightly flashing "Go This Way!" but He will guide us through prayer, Scripture, and the advice of capable people, including religious, civil, and medical authorities. The late Mother Angelica, the foundress of the Catholic media network EWTN, used to say, "Faith is one foot on the ground, one foot in the air, and a queasy feeling in the stomach." We put our trust in God and keep moving forward.

After one of my talks a few years ago, a woman came up to my book table with a suggestion regarding the word "surrender." She said perhaps "surrender" is a four-letter word, as in Mary's *fiat*, or yes, to the Lord. Wow! That was brilliant! I gave it a lot of thought then and am doing it more so now. Think about it. We're having a hard time surrendering to all the changes and restrictions that come with the coronavirus. Scary, yes, but don't they pale in comparison with what Mary, as a teenage girl, was asked to do over two thousand years ago?

Or how about the four-letter word "love," as in the love of God on the Cross? We need to get back to thinking about His sacrifice during more than just the Lenten and Easter seasons or when we have a crisis in our lives. If we believe that Jesus is Lord of Lords and truly King of Kings, when are we going to truly surrender to that incredible love and give Him the corona—the crown He so truly deserves?

What does "surrender" to God mean to you?

In relationship to the pandemic, what are you having a hard time surrendering (health concerns, financial issues, family matters)?

What are you hoping to learn and apply about your life and your relationship with God regarding coronavirus challenges?

6

CONQUERING
CORONAVIRUS

By Abandonment to the Will of God

*I know the plans I have for you, says the L*ORD*, plans for welfare and not for evil, to give you a future and a hope.*

—Jeremiah 29:11

"QUE SERA SERA" WAS a song made famous by actress and singer Doris Day. It soared to the top of the Billboard music charts in the mid-1950s after she sang it in the 1956 Alfred Hitchcock film *The Man Who Knew Too Much*. It was a song that was very familiar to me and the rest of my Italian American family, as it was also my grandmother Anna Tomeo's favorite song.

She would refer to the refrain, whenever one of us would get frustrated or angry about something unpleasant happening in our lives, reminding us that we can't predict the future or control it. Looking back now, and seeing things from a Christian versus a worldly perspective, I realize, without directly saying so, she was also trying to teach us a valuable faith lesson concerning God's will and providence.

> Que sera sera, whatever will be, will be.
> The future is not ours to see, que sera sera.

For the first few nights after my mother passed away, I had trouble sleeping. The temporary insomnia was no doubt due to my pain and frustration of not being able to give Mom what I believed was the proper send-off. The recording of all my disappointments kept playing over and over in my head.

Suddenly, and I'm sure it was the Holy Spirit, Grandma's favorite tune came to mind. "Whatever will be, will be." I realized there was immense grace in God's timing for both me and my mother.

Although I was able to be at my mom's side because of her critical state, all of the other residents were alone. No visitors allowed. I don't think I could have handled not seeing my mom or being able to connect only through phone calls. It would have been so emotionally draining for both of us to be apart physically for weeks, even months, on end.

My mother's passing was not a shock. She had been in and out of the hospital and rehab centers numerous times in the months before her death. She had been slowing down a great deal, and we knew it could happen at any time. God's timing in her death protected us from the pain of isolation that other residents of the rest home were suffering.

Truly, as we read in Job 1:21, "The LORD gave, and the LORD has taken away; blessed be the name of the LORD." For reasons we cannot fathom, God has allowed this pandemic to occur during our lifetime. It is what it is, or as Grandma Tomeo used to sing, "Whatever will be, will be." The future is, again, "not ours to see."

If we keep our eyes on Christ, the one sure thing we will see, although perhaps not the way we anticipate it, is God's grace being poured out upon us.

reflection

What are you doing to reach out to
those who might be isolated and alone
(and not just during the pandemic)?

How has God provided or shown
you examples of His grace during
these challenging times?

What lessons can you share with
others concerning the grace
that comes with suffering?

Who do you think most needs
to hear about this grace?

7

CONQUERING
CORONAVIRUS

Despite Material and Spiritual Obstacles

*And who knows whether you have not come
to the kingdom for such a time as this?*

—Esther 4:14

ALBERT EINSTEIN IS QUOTED as saying, "In the middle of difficulty lies opportunity." If that's the case, then, when it comes to growing in our faith and sharing it with others, we must have a boatload of opportunities in front of us.

One of my favorite books in the Old Testament is Esther. Queen Esther was a beautiful Jewish girl who saved her people from being wiped out. She was an orphan who became Queen of Persia around 475 B.C. Scripture tells us that King Ahasuerus loved her more than "all the other women and she found grace and favor in his sight" (Esther 2:17). She had a very good life by all accounts until she was asked to step outside her comfort zone to put the lives of her people before her own.

Her guardian, Mordecai, a devout Jew, refused to pay homage to one of the king's officials. As a result, the official devised a plot to destroy all the Jews in the kingdom. Mordecai learned of the plot and encouraged Esther to speak to the king on behalf of the Jewish people. The problem was that in the those days, no one, not even the king's precious Queen Esther, could enter his chambers without being summoned. To do so would almost certainly result in death. Even so, Mordecai impressed upon Esther that this moment might be the very reason God chose her to be queen in the first place:

If you keep silence at such a time as this, relief and deliverance will rise for the Jews from another quarter, but you and your father's house will perish. And who knows whether you have not come to the kingdom for such a time as this? (Esther 4:14)

Esther knew what she had to do. Before presenting herself to the king, she spent days in prayer. She also called for spiritual backup. She sent a message to the Jewish people, asking them to join her in prayer and fasting.

Go, gather all the Jews to be found in Susa, and hold a fast on my behalf, and neither eat nor drink for three days, night or day. I and my maids will also fast as you do. Then I will go to the king, though it is against the law; and if I perish, I perish. (Esther 4:16)

Here's a spoiler alert if you haven't read the entire book of Esther, which I highly encourage you to do: the queen wins over the king and saves her people. Esther had the courage, in the face of death, to do what needed to be done. She turned a major obstacle (a likely death sentence) into an opportunity, which, in turn, saved the lives of thousands of people.

While we may not be asked to put our physical lives on the line for the sake of others right now, there are plenty of people in the medical and law-enforcement fields who are doing just that. Already this virus has killed hundreds of doctors worldwide. In honor of their heroic efforts, we should be willing to do our part.

Let's revisit the inspirational video message of Fr. John Riccardo, who is hoping we won't turn our backs on the gift hidden in this noteworthy time in our lives:

As much as you and I might not have wanted it, you and I were born for this moment. So let us ask God to give us the grace to continue to hear what it is He is trying to say in these days, and let's pray for the courage to do what it is that He is asking of us.

We Christians have an eternal task before us right now. We're called to respond to the spiritual needs we see in our community. In these pages, we've already referenced studies showing an increased interest in prayer. If you're not quite convinced of the world's current hunger for God, here are a few other reports to ponder. A survey[11] of nearly twelve thousand adults by the Pew Research Center, from the end of March 2020, states that a majority of Americans are praying for an end to the pandemic, and that includes some who admit they rarely pray.

> The virus also has impacted Americans' religious behaviors. More than half of all U.S. adults (55%) say they have prayed for an end to the spread of coronavirus. Large majorities of Americans who pray daily (86%) and of U.S. Christians (73%) have taken to prayer during the outbreak — but so have some who say they seldom or never pray and people who say they do not belong to any religion (15% and 24%, respectively).

Raise your hand if you know someone, friend or relative, who has fallen away from his or her faith. It's very possible that your son, daughter, or neighbor is among those expressing, as this

---

[11] "Most Americans Say Coronavirus Outbreak Has Impacted Their Lives," Pew Research Center, March 30, 2020, www.pew-socialtrends.org/2020/03/30/most-americans-say-coronavirus-outbreak-has-impacted-their-lives/.

survey indicates, a new openness to God. The lack of in-person services has even resulted in worshippers looking for other ways to connect:

> A similar share (57%) reports having watched religious services online or on TV instead of attending in person. Together, four-in-ten regular worshippers appear to have *replaced* in-person attendance with virtual worship (saying that they have been attending less often but watching online instead).

In the March 31 edition of his weekly radio show, *Conversation with Cardinal Dolan*, New York's Cardinal Timothy Dolan says that ratings for online Mass at St. Patrick's Cathedral are skyrocketing after church doors in New York were shut in March because of coronavirus:

> I was given a report that now we have some thirty thousand people that watch the livestream. Isn't that phenomenal?

He added that some pastors are reporting a bigger audience on the livestream than at church when things were normal. He's hoping that this translates into a spiritual revival.

You don't have to be a Bible scholar or have a theology degree to get involved. Years ago, I heard a preacher say, "One of the most important aspects of being a Christian is just showing up." Given the hunger as well as the isolation being felt right now, there are plenty of ways to do just that.

A husband and wife team were concerned about elderly members living alone, so they got busy with an outreach program, among other things. Richard and Kristine Hass are members of St. Paul Street Evangelization, a Michigan-based organization dedicated to Catholic evangelization. According to the *Detroit Catholic* website, they normally, as you might have guessed based on the name of the ministry, take their evangelization efforts to the streets. Now that the street outreach involving setting up tables with Catholic books and literature, or handing out rosaries and prayer cards, has been postponed, they're working through their home parish to make deliveries of "food, medicine, and of course, prayer." The prayer and outreach happen by phone with a focus on the elderly. They were pleasantly surprised by the response.

> As much as we called concerned about their well-being, for many, their top priority was making sure our pastor and priests are well. Our 104-year-old parishioner wanted to make sure that the monsignor knew she was well and asked us to tell him not to worry because she is praying for him every day.

As grateful as the recipients of the calls were, so were the volunteers who called them. One volunteer said in an e-mail, "I will reach out to my new best friends next week." She said it was a joy talking to those on her list. The ministry had decided at the start that it wasn't a one-time thing, and as part of its call checklist, they made sure that callers extended the invitation to call again. That was a much-welcomed offer.

The laity are also helping with the online Masses being offered through the parish website. In the Diocese of Phoenix, members of the laity helped put together an online flip-book, *A Journey through Holy Week for Families*, a resource for celebrating Holy Week with loved ones. Other Catholics with theatrical gifts are lending their voice talents to recording Catholic children's books. The audio versions are then shared online.

These are just some examples, but they're no doubt what Pope Francis had in mind when he called for the creativity of love as part of an April 3 video message directed at families.[12]

> I can imagine you in your families, living an unusual life to avoid contagion. I am thinking of the liveliness of children and young people, who cannot go out, attend school, live their lives. I have in my heart all the families, especially those who have a loved one who is sick or who have unfortunately experienced mourning due to the coronavirus or other causes.... Let us try, if we can, to make the best use of this time: let us be generous; let us help those in need in our neighborhood; let us look out for the loneliest people, perhaps by telephone or social networks; let us pray to the Lord for those who are in difficulty in Italy and in the world. Even if we are isolated, thought and spirit can go far with the creativity of love. This is what is needed today: the creativity of love.

If you're wondering what you can do to make a difference, start with prayer. And in this case, I'm not just talking about any prayer. I'm speaking of a prayer written for a pandemic. It was part of another great Lenten homily I heard. It really puts the situation in perspective and hopefully will provide some ideas on how you can show the love of Christ in your own community.

---

[12] Devin Watkins, "Pope's Holy Week Message: 'Creativity of Love Can Overcome Isolation,'" Vatican News, April 3, 2020. www. vaticannews.va/en/pope/news/2020-04/pope-francis-holy-week-2020-message-coronavirus.html.

Prayer for a Pandemic
by Cameron Bellm

May we who are merely inconvenienced
Remember those whose lives are at stake.
May we who have no risk factors
Remember those most vulnerable.
May we who have the luxury of working from home
Remember those who must choose between
    preserving their health or making their rent.
May we who have the flexibility to care for
    our children when their schools close
Remember those who have no options.
May we who have to cancel our trips
Remember those that have no safe place to go.
May we who are losing our margin money
    in the tumult of the economic market
Remember those who have no margin at all.
May we who settle in for a quarantine at home
Remember those who have no home.
As fear grips our country,
Let us choose love.
During this time when we cannot
    physically wrap our arms around each other,
Let us yet find ways to be the loving
    embrace of God to our neighbors. Amen.

Ask God to put people in your path in need of support. It could be, as the pope said, something as simple as a phone call or an e-mail. Whatever you're called to do, as that Nike slogan says, "Just do it."

reflection

Do you see the pandemic as an obstacle or an opportunity? Why?

How can you "show up" and make a difference for someone in need as a result of the coronavirus? Discuss specific actions or areas of outreach where you feel you could best serve.

How has the virus affected your level or attitude of gratitude?

What are you most grateful for right now? How can you improve your attitude of gratitude?

8

CONQUERING
CORONAVIRUS

*Through Brave
Community
Service*

I can do all things in [Christ] who strengthens me.

—Philippians 4:13

IF WE'RE STILL BLESSED enough to be on this planet, God's not through with us. He's got work for us to do, and if there is anything I've learned along the way, it's that if God brings us to it, He will see us through it. Though none of us likes to suffer, if we're open to learning, our struggles can be our best teachers. By now, I hope and pray that this book has helped you to become aware of the lessons you've learned as well as given you the ability to view the coronavirus differently.

My friend and colleague Al Kresta has a great motto: "Look at everything through the lenses of Scripture and the teachings of the Catholic Church." If we do that, we will see things from a much bigger perspective, in light of both salvation and Church history. In other words, this isn't exactly our first rodeo. The coronavirus pandemic may be a mammoth crisis, but it's not larger than God, and He is longing for an invitation to help us conquer our fears, through Him.

As I was writing this book, a friend of mine sent me an anonymous reflection that highlighted the incredible works of mercy being undertaken by individuals, small businesses, churches, large corporations, families, and celebrities. The list, as you will see, goes on. It's entitled "We Got This," and from what little information I've been able to dig up, it apparently started to circulate among nurses and other medical personnel who are working to fight the virus. It's truly inspirational and helps us see what we can do when we put aside our fears and join together.

WE GOT THIS

- Carnival Cruise Line told President Trump, "We can match those big Navy hospital ships with some fully staffed cruise ships."
- GM and Ford said, "Hold our cars, watch this; by next week we can make ventilators where last week we were making cars."
- Construction companies said, "Here are masks for the medical staff and doctors."
- Restaurants and schools said, "We've got kitchens and staff; we can feed the kids."
- NHL and NBA players are writing checks to pay the arena staff during postponed seasons.
- Churches are holding online services and taking care of their members and community.
- Women and children are making homemade masks and handing out snacks to truckers.
- Breweries are making sanitizer out of their leftover ingredients.
- We thought we couldn't live without baseball, hockey, and NASCAR, or going to beaches, restaurants, or a bar. Instead, we're ordering takeout to help keep businesses alive.
- What they didn't count on was America saying, "Hold my beer, watch this."

- A Japanese admiral in the middle of the Pacific said it best in 1941: "I think we have awakened a sleeping giant."
- Give us a little more time, and we will be doing much better! Stop listening to the hysterical media. We are one nation, indivisible.

It would be naïve to say or think, however, that the good deeds being done by so many are going to wipe out all the polarization and toxicity in our nation.

That said, the nation and the world in general, reminiscent of the days following 9-11, are uniting. Do you think we can continue this unifying trend? A Gallup poll[13] taken fifteen years after America pulled together following the terrorist attacks showed that patriotism was at an all-time low. Sadly, the poll was released shortly before Independence Day in 2016:

As the nation prepares to celebrate Independence Day, 52% of U.S. adults say they are "extremely proud" to be Americans, a new low in Gallup's 16-year trend. Americans' patriotism spiked after 9/11, peaking at 70% in 2003, but has declined since, including an eight-percentage-point drop in early 2005 and a five-point drop since 2013.

The survey was cited in several articles, including foreign publications such as the United Kingdom's *Independent* newspaper.

The immediate aftermath of the attacks saw a nation come together—in acts of defiance and expressions of patriotism. Stores ran out of flags, millions donated blood,

[13] Jeffrey M. Jones, "New Low of 52% 'Extremely Proud' to Be Americans," Gallup, July 1, 2016, news.gallup.com/poll/193379/new-low-extremely-proud-americans.aspx.

thousands enlisted. There was political bipartisanship as Congress passed a $40 billion anti-terrorism and victim aid measure, three days after the attack. The words "United We Stand" were not just a throwaway motto but the foundation of how America intended to move on.

At the time that Gallup survey was conducted, we were in the middle of what we thought at the time were the nastiest national elections in our country's history. Since then, public discord and division have only increased. Yes, 9-11 showed us what we can do when we put differences aside to help our fellow man. Unfortunately, it's also shown us that we have short memories.

The coronavirus pandemic is larger than the attacks of September 11, 2001, which means that God is giving us an even larger opportunity this time to bring about change. He's calling us back to Himself yet again.

The only one we can change, however, with the help and grace of God, is the person we see in the mirror. Sure, we've got this, but only if we truly believe that God has got us, and we respond to His calling card today.

> Seek the LORD while he may be found, call upon him while he is near; let the wicked forsake his way, and the unrighteous man his thoughts; let him return to the LORD, that he might have mercy on him, and to our God, for he will abundantly pardon. (Isa. 55:6–7)

PERSONAL

reflection

What actions can you take to ensure
positive, long-term change in your personal
relationship with God and the Church?
Increased reception of the sacraments?
Scripture study? A stronger prayer life?

What do you think religious leaders
can do to prompt a revival among
Catholics and other Christians?

Are you willing to share the lessons
learned from your coronavirus challenges
or experiences? If so, how?

9

CONQUERING
CORONAVIRUS

*With Faith-
Filled
Creativity*

I will not leave you orphans; I will come to you.

—John 14:18, NABRE

"WHAT WENT THROUGH YOUR mind as you were reading the Gospel in front of rows and rows of empty pews?" That was just one of the many questions I asked my husband, Dominick, a deacon in the Archdiocese of Detroit, after he came home from serving at our parish's first livestreamed Mass—a service that countless parishes have made available since public gatherings of all varieties were canceled.

After thinking about it, he responded with a very serious tone in his voice: "It was both surreal and sad." Although he was grateful still to be able to serve, he went on to say that it is something he and other clergy could never have prepared for or imagined. The world has certainly seen its share of plagues. But there still isn't a seminary anywhere on God's green earth that has taught a modern-day course on how specifically to minister at a time such as this, when clergy are completely separated physically from their congregants and followers.

It's difficult enough to be in ministry these days. Church attendance for the past few years has been on a downward trend. More millennials and other adults are identifying as "nones"—those who have no religious identification whatsoever. And let's not forget the scandals that continue to plague both the Catholic and Evangelical churches, adding to an already extremely challenging and volatile environment.

Then the pandemic came along, and leaders were forced to do the unthinkable: shut the doors of their churches, for the common good. There was and still is a lot of pushback from those in the pews, with questions raised about the necessity of all the restrictions. The questions and concerns are certainly legitimate, given the severity of the situation, meaning no public Masses and services even during Holy Week, the most important week on the Christian calendar.

This is new territory for the Church, and given all the unknowns about COVID-19, the approach so far has been "better safe than sorry." Perhaps if we look at this with a "we're all in this together" view instead of an "us versus them" mentality, we'll all be much better off in the long run. I hope that sharing just a few of the remarkable stories concerning creative shepherds will ease the pain.

Despite their sadness and disappointment, many priests, bishops, Protestant pastors, and other evangelists are turning bushels and baskets of sour lemons into a thirst-quenching lemonade by coming up with all sorts of creative ways to reach the faithful as well as anyone else who needs encouragement right now. And they're truly thinking outside the box when it comes to being Christlike and letting congregants know they're not alone.

One of my favorite examples comes straight from one of the major epicenters of the virus: northern Italy and the outskirts of Milan. That's where Fr. Giuseppe Corbari decided he needed to see the faces of the faithful somehow, even though they were not allowed to step one foot inside the church. So he asked them to send him selfies. He then printed up dozens of the photos and pasted the pictures on the pews so he could look at their *volti belli* (beautiful faces) as he celebrated Mass.

During a radio interview,[14] the president of Franciscan University of Steubenville, Ohio, Fr. Dave Pivonka, fought back tears as he tried to describe to my listeners what the separation has been like for him and other religious leaders:

> It's a cross like no other, one I never ever imagined the Lord would ask me to carry, and yet I am also experiencing Jesus during this. Who here at this university has not prayed, "Lord, if this cup could pass," but that is exactly the prayer that Jesus made, and the reality is that this is the cup that the Lord is offering us. And I never imagined that … we would have to do this, but the Lord has been so close and so personal. And yet that is the mystery of our Faith, right? Our salvation comes about first through obedience. Jesus was obedient to His Father. And we, as priests, we must be obedient. We can't pick and choose.

Fr. Pivonka stressed that part of our job, when separated from Christ in the Eucharist, is to be honest with ourselves in admitting that being separated hurts.

> It's okay to feel hurt and empty. If the Eucharist really is, as the Catholic Church proclaims, the summit of our Faith, nothing quite satisfies. Yes, I think it's an invitation for us really to discover Jesus in the Scriptures. The Scriptures are the living Word of God, and He is present, and we can build our life on that and get direction there, and wisdom, insight, and consolation. That's all wonderful, beautiful, and good, but there is something unique

[14] *Catholic Connection*, April 3, 2020, www.avemariaradio.net.

about the Eucharist so that longing and that sadness, that desire, is not going to be satisfied by anything other than the Eucharist. And that's okay.

Fr. Pivonka started a white-ribbon campaign on his college campus to remind students and faculty that they're not alone. In a March 2020 opinion piece[15] for the Catholic News Agency, Pivonka described how ribbons have long been a sign of remembrance:

> They tell the world that we have not forgotten someone: a prisoner, a soldier, or a sick friend. I've tied a white ribbon onto the door of Christ the King Chapel, as well as the Portiuncula Chapel here at Franciscan University to remind our community that their priests and their God have not forgotten them. I've invited my friends who are priests and bishops to do the same. They, in turn, are inviting more priests and bishops to join us. My hope is that as Catholics walk or drive past their churches, they will see those white ribbons and know their priests are praying for them and waiting for the day we can fling open those doors to welcome them back inside.

Nearly 350 miles northwest of Steubenville, in the Michigan diocese of Lansing, Fr. Mark Rutherford, the pastor of St. Mary's parish in the small town of Williamston, took to the skies, some ten thousand feet in the air, to share God's healing and protection not only with the members of his church but with the entire

---

[15] Father Dave Pivonka, TOR, "White Ribbons: 'I Will Never Forget You,'" Catholic News Agency, March 31, 2020. www.catholicnewsagency.com/column/white-ribbons-i-will-never-forget-you-4143.

diocese. He decided to conduct a Eucharistic procession: a public witness recognizing and venerating or honoring Jesus in the Holy Eucharist. Normally such events are done through city streets for special liturgical events, with priests carrying the Eucharist in a special monstrance or receptacle and leading a public procession.

> This isn't anything new [Fr. Rutherford told me during a radio interview on *Catholic Connection*]. This has been part of the tradition of the Church from the beginning. Some of the beautiful stories I love reading, for example, include one about a priest in 1656, as the Spanish plague was approaching a small city near Naples, Italy. In response, Fr. Paolo Franco led villagers in a procession up nearby Monte Castello, bearing the Eucharist before them in a monstrance. Once the procession reached the top, he blessed the entire village from above. Miraculously, the plague spared the city. To this day, the town organizes multiple Eucharistic processions in commemoration of this first one. So there are a lot of stories in the Church's history of priests and bishops doing creative processions in response to a threat, whether plague, fire, flood, or something other.

Fr. Rutherford took off in a chartered aircraft from Livingston County airport in Howell, Michigan, flying over all ten counties in the Lansing Diocese. As Fr. Rutherford explained in a video posted on the diocesan website (dioceseoflansing.org), he prayed throughout the journey, blessing all below, assisted by a seminarian.

> Our God heals, and He loves healing, He takes delight in healing; all we have to do is ask. So one of the purposes of

this procession around the diocese is to ask our heavenly Father to heal us of COVID-19, to heal all of those who currently have it, praying that our heavenly Father heals them and restores them. We also prayed for the few people that have already died as a result of COVID. We prayed for the repose of their souls and for their families.

It's not a stretch to say there probably isn't a church or a synagogue around that isn't taking advantage of the blessing of modern technology by offering services, retreats, and Scripture studies online, with a lot of those events carried live on the Internet. They could have stopped there. But as you've just read, there are all sorts of outreach initiatives being made. Whether it's plastering photos of parishioners all over the pews, the gentle reminder of a white-ribbon campaign, or a bold procession ten thousand feet above the earth, religious leaders are emulating Christ. To reference a well-known Motown classic, there really isn't a mountain, or more precisely, sky, high enough to keep them and the good Lord, from getting to you and to me.

PERSONAL
reflection

––––––––––––

How have you seen priests, religious,
or other ministers reaching out
to the faith community?

What does their outreach mean to you,
especially at a time when attending
religious services in person is prohibited?

How have the examples of outreach
impacted your efforts to reach out
to others during difficult times?

What could you be doing to
reach out to others in need?

10

By Preaching the Gospel in Words and Deeds

*If I preach the gospel, this is no reason for me
to boast, for an obligation has been imposed on
me, and woe to me if I do not preach it!*

—1 Corinthians 9:16, NABRE

THERE IS ADVICE OFTEN attributed to the much-loved St. Francis of Assisi: "Preach the gospel always! When necessary use words."

Given all the selfless acts of charity, sacrifice, and goodwill that continue to occur as a result of the pandemic, there is no doubt that quite a few folks are preaching the gospel, even if they don't realize it. They're performing not only Corporal Works of Mercy, as mentioned earlier, by meeting the physical needs of a neighbor or loved one. They're also performing Spiritual Works of Mercy, which paragraph 2447 of the *Catechism of the Catholic Church* defines as "charitable actions by which we come to the aid of our neighbor" in spiritual necessities, those being focused on getting a soul to Heaven.

The Spiritual Works of Mercy include counseling the doubtful and comforting the sorrowful. You may not think that making a meal for an elderly neighbor or offering to pray with someone over the phone is all that extraordinary, but given the level of fear and doubt so many souls are suffering, you are truly making a difference and bringing the light of Christ to a world that today is shadowed in darkness as a result of this pandemic.

It's downright exhilarating and inspiring when you stop and think about all the goodness being spread, all the seeds of hope being planted today. I don't exactly have a green thumb, nor do

I need to have a degree in horticulture to know that seeds don't grow into beautiful, fruitful plants or trees unless they're regularly watered. Now is the time to think and pray about how you and I can help the already countless corporal and spiritual acts of mercy grow into a gorgeous garden of light for God.

What can we do more, better, or differently to spread the Faith?

Recall for a moment the parable of the sower in the Gospel. There Jesus tells of a farmer who scatters lots of seeds. Some fall upon rich, fertile soil and grow into healthy plants; others fall on shallow, rocky soil, where the sun quickly scorches the roots of the few plants that manage to sprout there.

That parable is about us.

Decades of prosperity and what seemed likely to be decades more of it have hardened our hearts against God and His gospel. What need have we of Him when we have good jobs, Botox, McDonald's, NASCAR, cheap cruises, and, best of all, the Super Bowl?

Suddenly—and amazingly, in just a matter of weeks—all those ordinary elements of our days and ways have either been threatened or entirely denied to us. The stock market has crashed and we are left to stand helplessly by as even our government—the most powerful in the world—cannot stop this killing virus that is seizing not just anonymous persons on some foreign soil but George, the quiet fellow who sits next to you in the call center, or Louanne, the sweet widow next door.

Even more than the events of 9-11, and by means of events like these, the coronavirus has shattered the complacency of millions of souls around the world, breaking up the hard, crusted soil of their souls and rendering them more like the fertile ground that, in the parable of the sower, was able to receive the Word of God.

In an e-mail sent to his archdiocese on Holy Saturday 2020, Archbishop Allen Vigneron of Detroit directed our attention to precisely this opportunity, which we must not let pass:

> We still must be about evangelization. That is always our mission. This is a providential time for us to witness to our sure confidence in Jesus as Lord of history to manifest to the world that we face this challenge with unshakable trust that the Lord will sustain us. *But we need to turn back to Holy Trinity + Blessed Mother*

If you've picked up this book, I would venture to say that you already have some level of faith or, at least, as a result of the coronavirus, have a newfound interest in spiritual matters. Know that God loves you right where you are. He also loves you too much to leave you there.

This is, as Archbishop Vigneron said, "a providential time." It's a time for you to grow individually in your relationship with God. It's also a time for each of us to help others to do the same. You'll be amazed at what God can do with just one small seed, one yes softly but sincerely spoken.

Let us then heed the words of Jesus, who gave us the Great Commission of evangelization, which is found in Matthew 28:19–20:

> Go therefore and make disciples of all nations, baptizing them in the name of the Father and of the Son and of the Holy Spirit, teaching them to observe all that I have commanded you; and lo, I am with you always, to the close of the age.

In what ways have you already
followed the words of St. Francis in
preaching the gospel always?

What led you to perform these Corporal
and Spiritual Works of Mercy?

How do you think the coronavirus
has impacted your faith in the
short and long term?

What can you do to respond
to Jesus' Great Commission of
evangelization during this crisis?

How will you continue not only
to plant but to tend to the seeds of
faith after the pandemic is over?

11

CONQUERING CORONAVIRUS

In Your Own Special Circumstances

May the God of peace . . . equip you with everything good that you
may do his will, working in you that which is pleasing in his sight,
through Jesus Christ; to whom be glory for ever and ever. Amen.

—Hebrews 13:20–21

HELP FOR
THOSE WHO HAVE BEEN DIAGNOSED
WITH CORONAVIRUS

God Knows Exactly How You Feel

The unknowns connected with this virus add to your fear and anxiety, especially if you have been diagnosed with it. As you seek medical treatment and work toward recovery, take comfort in the fact that Jesus knows how you feel, quite literally. The emotional and physical trials you're going through were also felt by Him as He experienced His Passion on Good Friday. Bring all your pain and suffering and lay it at the foot of Cross, asking for Christ's help in carrying this burden. He is the Great Physician and will not abandon any of us in our time of need.

HELPFUL THINGS YOU CAN DO

- Ask for prayer and assistance from your parish and medical experts. In addition to proper medical attention, spiritual and emotional support are keys to recovery.
- Stay close to Jesus and the Church by taking advantage of all the faith-based resources being made available, including online retreats, livestreaming of the Mass, and Catholic radio and TV. Protestant services are available for non-Catholics.
- Spend more time with God in daily Scripture reading. This will also keep you in touch with the universal Church and help you feel a sense of community.

- Stay close to loved ones through technology. Even something as basic as phone calls can serve as important lifelines. Many dioceses and parishes already have volunteers in place conducting outreach to those affected. Let your parish or congregation know that you welcome the contact.
- As you pray for healing, also pray to discover how God wants you to use this trial to help others who are suffering. Imagine the comfort you might bring to someone else by sharing your thoughts and experience.

PRAYERS FOR PEACE AND CONSOLATION

Coronavirus Victims' Prayer

God, our Father, mercifully look upon Your people who come to You, and grant, through the intercession of St. Rosalie, who turned away from earthly delights to the joys of contemplation, that we may be delivered from all harm here on earth and one day be welcomed into the Kingdom of Heaven. Amen.

A Prayer in Time of Sickness

Jesus, You suffered and died for us. You understand suffering. Teach me to understand my suffering as You do; to bear it in union with You; to offer it with You to atone for my sins and to bring Your grace to souls in need. Calm my fears; increase my trust. May I gladly accept Your holy will and become more like You in trial. If it be Your will, restore me to health so that I may work for Your honor and glory and the salvation of all. Amen.

**A Coronavirus Protection Prayer to the
Virgin Mary by Pope Francis**

*Mary, you shine continuously on our journey as a sign of salvation
and hope. We entrust ourselves to you, Health of the Sick. At the
foot of the Cross you participated in Jesus' pain, with steadfast
faith. We are certain that you will provide, so that, as you did
at Cana of Galilee, joy and feasting might return after this
moment of trial. Help us, Mother of Divine Love, to conform
ourselves to the Father's will and to do what Jesus tells us.*

SCRIPTURE PASSAGES TO CALM YOUR FEARS AND RESTORE YOUR COURAGE

- **Hebrews 4:15:** We have not a high priest who is unable to sympathize with our weaknesses, but one who in every respect has been tempted as we are, yet without sinning.
- **Jeremiah 30:17:** I will restore health to you, and your wounds I will heal, says the LORD, because they have called you an outcast: "It is Zion, for whom no one cares!"
- **Exodus 15:26:** For I am the LORD, your healer.

WORDS OF WISDOM AND ENCOURAGEMENT

- "When God is with us, we do not need to be afraid." —Bl. Pier Giorgio Frassati
- "Should you shield the canyons from the windstorms you would never see the true beauty of their carvings." —Elisabeth Kübler-Ross

- "Don't look at your weaknesses. Realize instead that in Christ crucified you can do everything."—St. Catherine of Siena

OTHER HELPFUL RESOURCES

- **EWTN (Eternal Word Television Network):** www.ewtn.com
- **How to pray the Rosary:** www.ewtn.com/legacy/devotionals/prayers/rosary/how_to.htm
- **Pray an act of perfect contrition:** www.catholicnewsagency.com/news/cant-go-to-confession-during-coronavirus-consider-an-act-of-perfect-contrition-26717
- **U.S. coronavirus website:** www.coronavirus.gov
- **Centers for Disease Control:** www.cdc.gov/coronavirus
- **Catholic Medical Association *Doctor, Doctor* podcast:** www.cathmed.org/resources/doctor-doctor/

HELP FOR
THE UNEMPLOYED AND
FINANCIALLY CHALLENGED

God Will Send You Pennies from Heaven

Losing your job can be frightening and emotionally debilitating. I know. I've been there on the unemployment line, and more than once. We all have bills to pay, mouths to feed, and beyond those necessities are our commitments, goals, and pride in doing our work well. Don't be afraid to reach out for help, including spiritual guidance, emotional support, and financial assistance. Begin on your knees, asking God to guide you. Although it might not look very hopeful right now, this could be an opportunity in disguise. Be open to what God may have in store for you. It may be bigger and better than anything you've ever dreamed of.

HELPFUL THINGS YOU CAN DO

- Take the proper steps to investigate and receive financial support, if necessary, whether on an individual or small-business basis. Log on to your state's website and file for unemployment and review other help available.
- See your current situation as a gain as opposed to a loss. You have been gifted with the time to grow closer to Christ. How about taking that online Bible study you were thinking about or listening to more faith-based presentations? Fill yourself with messages of hope, and make the most of the time that has been given to you.

- Before you begin the search for new job opportunities, take a badly needed break. Step back and give yourself some time, at least several days, to heal before applying for a new position. A layoff can be emotionally debilitating. You need time to pray, to reevaluate, and to regain your confidence.
- Reach out to others in need, including those who might be worse off than you. Volunteer to make calls to at-risk individuals, such as the elderly in your neighborhood. Call your parish and find out how else you might be of service. Studies show that volunteering can reduce stress, reduce the risk of depression, and help us stay mentally and physically fit. In other words, you get a lot more than you give.
- Be open to stepping out of your "professional" comfort zone to consider how your talents and gifts might be applied differently in your next position. Is there something you've wanted to do or felt God calling you to do? Continue to seek His guidance in prayer, asking for the ability to be open to what God might have in store.

PRAYERS FOR PEACE AND CONSOLATION

Prayer in Times of Financial Troubles

Dear Lord, help me to find firm ground in this shaky economy. As I seek work and assistance, give me strength not to be anxious when I seem to be going nowhere; give me patience not to despair when things look bleak; give me serenity to know You are here with me, helping me to carry my crosses each day; so that I may do Your will, for the salvation of souls and for my eternal life. Amen.

Prayer for Employment
God, our Father, I turn to You, seeking Your divine help and guidance as I look for suitable employment. I need Your wisdom to guide my footsteps along the right path and to lead me to find the proper things to say and do in this situation. I wish to use the gifts and talents You have given me, but I need the opportunity to do so with gainful employment. Do not abandon me, dear Father, in this search; rather, grant me this favor I seek, so that I may return to You with praise and thanksgiving for Your gracious assistance. Grant this through Christ, our Lord. Amen.

Prayer to Be Able to Provide for My Family
Dear St. Joseph, you were faced with the responsibility of providing the necessities of life for Jesus and Mary. Look down with fatherly compassion upon me in my anxiety because of my present inability to support my family. Please help me find gainful employment very soon, so that this great burden of concern will be lifted from my heart and that I will soon be able to provide for those whom God has entrusted to my care. Help me guard against discouragement, so that I may emerge from this trial spiritually enriched and with even greater blessings from God. Amen.

Prayer to St. Jude, the Patron Saint of Impossible Causes (Health, Finances, Housing, Jobs, Relationships, etc.)
St. Jude, glorious apostle, faithful servant and friend of Jesus, the Church honors and invokes you universally as the patron of difficult and desperate cases. Pray for me, who am so miserable. Make use, I implore you, of that particular privilege accorded to you to bring visible and speedy help where help was almost despaired of. Come to my assistance in this great need, that

*I may receive the consolation and help of Heaven in all my
necessities, tribulations, and sufferings, particularly (here make
your request) and that I may bless God with you and all the
elect throughout all eternity. I promise you, O blessed St. Jude,
to be ever mindful of this great favor; and I will never cease
to honor you as my special and powerful patron and do all in
my power to encourage devotion to you. St. Jude, pray for
us and for all who honor you and invoke your aid. Amen.*

SCRIPTURE PASSAGES TO CALM YOUR FEARS AND RESTORE YOUR COURAGE

- **Proverbs 3:5–6:** Trust in the LORD with all your heart, and do not rely on your own insight. In all your ways acknowledge him, and he will make straight your paths.
- **Psalm 9:9–10:** The LORD is a stronghold for the oppressed, a stronghold in times of trouble.

WORDS OF WISDOM AND ENCOURAGEMENT

- "Pray as though everything depended on God. Work as though everything depended on you." —St. Augustine of Hippo
- "Pray, hope, and don't worry." —St. Pio of Pietrelcina
- "Worry is a weakness from which very few of us are entirely free. We must be on guard against this most insidious enemy of our peace of soul. Instead, let us foster confidence in God, and thank Him ahead of time for whatever He chooses to send us." —Bl. Solanus Casey

OTHER HELPFUL RESOURCES

- **St. Joseph the Worker Novena:** www.ewtn.com/catholicism/devotions/novena-to-st-joseph-304
- **Compass Catholic:** www.compasscatholic.org/
- **Coronavirus Aid, Relief, and Economic Security (CARES) Act:** www.usa.gov/disaster-financial-help
- **Small Business Administration:** www.sba.gov
- **How to file for Unemployment:** www.usa.gov/unemployment
- **U.S. Government Economy/Jobs website:** www.whitehouse.gov/issues/economy-jobs

HELP FOR FAMILY MEMBERS OF PERSONS DIAGNOSED WITH CORONAVIRUS

Pray Together to Stay Together

By now, you probably know someone who has been diagnosed with the coronavirus, possibly someone in your immediate family. As scary as this is, you're not alone. Joining together spiritually, leaning on Christ and your faith, is the first and one of the most important things you can do in getting through this trial. There is a long list of helpful links and resources provided here to help you stay strong as you tend to the needs of loved ones. Combining regular prayer and solid medical advice can make a difference. It's encouraging to note that medical professionals are focusing more attention on the impact of prayer on physical health. Rev. John K. Graham, a doctor and Episcopal priest, told CatholicPhilly.com that prayer

> affects every parameter that you can measure: blood pressure, cholesterol level, every chemical measure including stress/cortisol in the body.... Prayer is the foundational spiritual practice for almost everyone, even those who say they are not religious. If (the nonreligious) have a child who is ill or they are going into the operating room, they still pray. Sometimes that's called the "foxhole prayer," but I wouldn't diminish it. If you're at your desperate end of things, you'll turn to someone greater than yourself.

HELPFUL THINGS YOU CAN DO

- If your loved ones are separated from you because of the virus, send them spiritual resources, including prayer cards and other inspirational materials. Sending a Mass card, for example, lets them know they're covered in prayer.
- Record a special video message or make the most of technology by having regular FaceTime visits. My husband and I are very close to our young twin grand-nieces. Even though we are less than an hour apart, the virus restrictions have kept us separated. My nephew and his wife have been very good about uploading daily videos that are helping us deal with our separation.
- If someone in your home is ill, leave special notes on the food tray outside his or her door, and keep connected by phone and text. One married couple shared with me how the phone was a lifeline as it allowed the wife to check frequently on her husband while keeping a safe distance. She also let him how much she missed him and reminded him to get his rest and take his medication.
- Make prayer for a loved one struggling with the virus a family activity. Come together daily to pray for healing.
- Preparing meals and delivering them to other persons in need, while following, of course, all the CDC health regulations, can be a real pick-me-up for a friend or a family member. A priest friend of mine was recently quarantined. He sent me an e-mail hinting that he wouldn't mind receiving one of my famous Italian meals. I dropped off macaroni, homemade meatballs,

and chicken soup on his porch. And the smile I saw through the front door was worth the extra time in the kitchen.

PRAYERS FOR PEACE AND CONSOLATION

A Parent's Prayer

Loving God, You are the giver of all we possess, the source of all of our blessings. We thank and praise You. Thank You for the gift of our children. Help us to set boundaries for them and yet encourage them to explore. Give us the strength and courage to treat each day as a fresh start. May our children come to know You, the one true God, and Jesus Christ, whom You have sent. May Your Holy Spirit help them to grow in faith, hope, and love, so they may know peace, truth, and goodness. May their ears hear Your voice. May their eyes see Your presence in all things. May their lips proclaim Your Word. May their hearts be Your dwelling place. May their hands do works of charity. May their feet walk in the way of Jesus Christ, Your Son and our Lord. Amen.

Blessing Over Your Children

You can say the above prayer and end with a blessing upon the forehead, making the Sign of the Cross and saying,

"May God bless you and protect you in the name of the Father, and of the Son, and of the Holy Spirit. Amen."

SCRIPTURE PASSAGES TO CALM YOUR FEARS AND RESTORE YOUR COURAGE

- **Psalm 127:3–5:** Sons are a heritage from the LORD, the fruit of the womb a reward.
- **Matthew 18:10:** See that you do not despise one of these little ones; for I tell you that in heaven their angels always behold the face of my Father who is in heaven.
- **Psalm 138:8:** The LORD will fulfil his purpose for me; thy steadfast love, O LORD, endures for ever. Do not forsake the work of thy hands.

WORDS OF WISDOM AND ENCOURAGEMENT

- "Whatever you do for your family, your children, your husband, your wife, you do for God. All we do, our prayers, our work, our suffering, is for Jesus." —St. Teresa of Calcutta
- "Teach us to give and not count the cost." —St. Ignatius of Loyola
- "God doesn't want us to rescue our children. He's the Rescuer." —Elizabeth Musser, *Words Unspoken*

OTHER HELPFUL RESOURCES

- **Women of Grace online studies for women:** www.studies.womenofgrace.com
- **Scott Hahn/St. Paul Center online studies:** www.stpaulcenter.com/studies-tools/online-studies/
- **Avila Institute School of Spiritual Formation:** www.avila-institute.org/spiritual-formation/
- **Catholic Medical Association *Doctor, Doctor* podcast:** www.cathmed.org/resources/doctor-doctor/
- **American College of Pediatricians:** www.acpeds.org/parents
- **Dr. Ray Guarendi, *The Doctor Is In*:** www.DrRay.com
- **Focus on the Family:** www.focusonthefamily.com
- **Institute for Marital Healing:** www.maritalhealing.com
- **KidsHealth:** kidshealth.org/en/parents/coronavirus.html

HELP FOR
THE ELDERLY AND OTHERS
AT HIGH RISK

You're Not Alone

Those of you who are elderly or suffer from preexisting conditions are carrying quite a burden, as you are among the groups of individuals at greater risk than the general public. You have an abundance of prayers, love, and support. Even if shut-downs, along with social-distancing regulations, keep you from being in the physical presence of your loved ones, know that you are close at heart, not forgotten, and that the Lord has you in the palm of His hand.

HELPFUL THINGS YOU CAN DO

- If you live alone, reach out to your parish or local church, particularly if they haven't reached out to you already. Let them know that you welcome their prayers and whatever other types of outreach they have available.
- Don't ever think of yourself as a burden and ignore a health concern you might have. Keep in close contact with your immediate family and let them know how you're feeling, both physically and emotionally.
- Stay connected with the larger faith community by tuning in to Catholic radio and TV. In addition to daily Mass and the Rosary, Catholic media (especially

EWTN Global Catholic TV and Radio Network) is
offering special programming addressing the pandemic
from a Godly perspective, as are many Protestant media
outlets.

- Display religious images in your home. This will remind
  you of God's love and protection.
- Remind friends and loved ones that "window" visits are
  truly special. Recall the story I shared of the woman
  who made window visits to my mother's assisted-living
  facility. Her simple act of kindness helped me through a
  very difficult time, and I'm sure it had the same impact
  on the residents.

PRAYERS FOR PEACE AND CONSOLATION

Prayer for the Sick and for Seniors

*All praise and glory are Yours, Lord our God, for You have called
us to serve You and one another in love. Bless our sick today so
that they may bear their illness in union with Jesus' sufferings, and
restore them quickly to health. Bless those who have grown old in
Your service and give them courage and strength in their faith. Lead
us all to eternal glory. We ask this through our Lord Jesus Christ,
Your Son, who lives and reigns with You and the Holy Spirit, one
God, forever and ever. Amen.
Mother of Perpetual Help, pray for us.*

Prayer of the Elderly

*Dear Lord, as my life declines and my energies decrease,
more than ever hold me by Your power, that I may not offend
You, but daily increase in Your love. Give me strength to
work in Your service till the last day of my life. Help me ever
to have an increasing dread of venial sin, or whatever would
cause the slightest withdrawal of Your love. All day long, and
at night, keep me close to Your heart; and should I die, ere
the morning breaks, may I go rejoicing in that vision of Your
entrancing beauty, never to be separated from You. Amen.*

SCRIPTURE PASSAGES TO CALM YOUR FEARS AND RESTORE YOUR COURAGE

- **Isaiah 46:4:** Even to your old age I am He, and to gray hairs I will carry you. I have made, and I will bear; I will carry and will save.
- **1 Timothy 5:1–2:** Do not rebuke an older man but exhort him as you would a father; treat younger men like brothers, older women like mothers, younger women like sisters, in all purity.
- **Leviticus 19:32:** You shall rise up before the hoary head, and honor the face of an old man, and you shall fear your God: I am the LORD.

WORDS OF WISDOM AND ENCOURAGEMENT

- "Let us touch the dying, the poor, the lonely, and the unwanted according to the graces we have received, and let us not be ashamed or slow to do the humble work." —St. Teresa of Calcutta
- "The ultimate test of your greatness is the way you treat every human being." —St. John Paul II
- "Do not forget that true love sets no conditions; it does not calculate or complain, but simply loves." —St. John Paul II

OTHER HELPFUL RESOURCES

- **EWTN (the Eternal Word Television Network):** www.ewtn.com
- **How to pray the Rosary:** www.ewtn.com/legacy/devotionals/prayers/rosary/how_to.htm
- **Pray an act of perfect contrition:** www.catholicnewsagency.com/news/cant-go-to-confession-during-coronavirus-consider-an-act-of-perfect-contrition-26717
- **How to pray the Divine Mercy Chaplet:** https://www.thedivinemercy.org/message/devotions/pray-the-chaplet
- **Put an image of the Divine Mercy in your room:** www.thedivinemercy.org/message/devotions/image
- **Centers for Disease Control:** www.cdc.gov/aging
- **National Association of Area Agencies on Aging:** www.n4a.org

HELP FOR HEALTH-CARE WORKERS AND FIRST RESPONDERS

You Are Heroes among Us

On even a good day, you have it tough. Unless someone has walked in your shoes, facing this pandemic on the frontlines in the myriad ways you do, it's hard to imagine what you are going through. You have so many unknowns on your plate. And while caring for everyone else impacted by the virus, you're working untold hours and often putting yourself in harm's way. Thank you for your courage. Hopefully these activities will be helpful in replenishing you. Know that the Great Physician is watching over you and aware of the sacrifices you're making.

HELPFUL THINGS YOU CAN DO

- Listen to Christian music or other beautiful music — if possible, while at work. Studies show music can be an aid in reducing stress and lowering anxiety.
- If needed, take advantage of support available for medical professionals and others in risk- and stress-filled work like yours. Most medical facilities offer confidential guidance or assistance programs.
- Ask your loved ones to pray for your protection daily.
- When at home, take a break from the 24/7 newsfeeds and gavel-to-gavel coverage of the pandemic.

- Seek out fellow Christian workers in your field and establish times when you might meet for regular prayer and support.

PRAYERS FOR PEACE AND CONSOLATION

Prayer of Nurses and Health-Care Professionals
Dear Lord, please give me strength, to face the day ahead.
Dear Lord, please give me courage, as I approach each hurting bed.
Dear Lord, please give me wisdom with every word I speak.
Dear Lord, please give me patience, as I comfort the sick and weak.
Dear Lord, please give me assurance, as the day slips into night,
that I have done the best I can, that I have done what's right.

Prayer for First Responders
Please God, grant them courage when times are bleak.
Grant them strength when they feel weak.
Grant them comfort when they feel all alone.
And most of all, God, please bring them all home.

A Coronavirus Prayer for Health-Care Workers
Holy Spirit, we thank You for the advancements that have led to improving the health of so many. We beg You to inspire new breakthroughs in overcoming the coronavirus and all serious flu viruses. Protect, we pray, health-care professionals from the illnesses they are treating, and make them instruments of Your healing. Amen.

SCRIPTURE PASSAGES TO CALM YOUR FEARS AND RESTORE YOUR COURAGE

- **Luke 10:34:** [He] went to him and bound up his wounds, pouring on oil and wine; then he set him on his own beast and brought him to an inn, and took care of him.
- **1 Corinthians 6:19–20:** Do you not know that your body is a temple of the Holy Spirit within you, which you have from God? You are not your own; you were bought with a price. So glorify God in your body.
- **Colossians 4:14:** Luke, the beloved physician, sends greetings. (NABRE)

WORDS OF WISDOM AND ENCOURAGEMENT

- "Miracles are not contrary to nature, only to what we know about nature." —St. Augustine of Hippo
- "Turn to God. Believe in God. Trust Him for a miracle." —St. Pio of Pietrelcina

OTHER HELPFUL RESOURCES

- **Catholic Medical Association:** www.cathmed.org
- **St. Luke, patron saint of physicians:** www.ewtn.com/catholicism/saints/luke-674
- **St. Gianna Beretta Molla, patron saint of physicians:** www.ewtn.com/catholicism/saints/gianna-beretta-molla-589
- **St. Agatha, patron saint of nurses:** www.ewtn.com/catholicism/library/st-agatha-virgin-and-martyr-5164
- **CMA with COVID resources for doctors:** www.cathmed.org/programs-resources
- **Nurses for Life:** www.nursesforlife.org
- **Catholic therapists:** www.catholictherapists.com
- *Linacre Quarterly:* www.cathmed.org/programs-resources/cma-resources/linacre-quarterly

HELP FOR CHURCH LEADERS AND THE LAY FAITHFUL

We Are in This with You

We're all feeling the pain of separation right now. Whether you're a religious or a member of the lay faithful, what we're going through is unprecedented in our lifetime. God did not cause this current pandemic. For whatever reason, in His great wisdom, He is allowing this to happen now.

For those of you who are priests, pastors, deacons, and other religious leaders, know that you're making a real difference in the unique ways you continue to bring Christ to your people. For the laity, let's continue to reach out and help our leaders build up the Body of Christ when they need it most. For those of us normally in the pews, let's also think outside the box and be creative in ways we can join together virtually. Perhaps it's an opportunity for all of us to grow closer to Jesus and His Church and be more appreciative of everything that our Faith has to offer. In the meantime, let's help each other share the abundance of resources that have been created for us to stay connected and to grow in our relationship with God.

HELPFUL THINGS YOU CAN DO

- Get your family involved with creating a personal card or message that can be delivered to your parish or diocesan office, or your pastor's residence.

- If you are in a leadership role, continue your many fine efforts to reach out through websites, online presentations, retreats, and prayers. Many bishops are reporting large increases in the number of Catholics and others watching, for example, livestreamed Masses. Take comfort in the fact that your efforts are feeding your flock.
- Keep your faith community connected through group texts, e-mail blasts, and so forth, to remind them of events available.
- Collect and share positive stories of people helping people. Post them on social media and share in social media groups and on other platforms.
- Move your staff meetings, Bible studies, and prayer groups online. This is a great way not only to keep in touch but to help others feel productive and involved during a time with so many unknowns.

PRAYERS FOR PEACE AND CONSOLATION

Prayer for Church Leaders

Lord Jesus Christ, watch over the leaders in Your Church. Keep them faithful to their vocation and to the proclamation of Your message. Teach them to recognize and interpret the signs of the times. Strengthen them with the gifts of the Spirit, and help them to serve Your people, especially the poor and the lowly. Give them a vivid sense of Your presence in the world and a knowledge of how to show it to others. Amen.

Prayer for Priests and Pastors

Gracious and loving God, we thank You for the gift of our priests and pastors. Through them, we experience Your presence in the sacraments. Help them to be strong in their vocation. Set their souls on fire with love for Your people. Grant them the wisdom, understanding, and strength they need to follow in the footsteps of Jesus. Inspire them with the vision of Your Kingdom. Give them the words they need to spread the gospel. Allow them to experience joy in their ministry. Help them to become instruments of Your divine grace. We ask this through Jesus Christ, who lives and reigns as our Eternal Priest. Amen.

Prayer of St. Francis

Lord, make me an instrument of Your peace; where there is hatred, let me sow love; where there is injury, pardon; where there is doubt, faith; where there is despair, hope; where there is darkness, light; and where there is sadness, joy. Divine Master, grant that I may not so much seek to be consoled as to console; to be understood, as to understand; to be loved, as to love; for it is in giving that we receive, it is in pardoning that we are pardoned, and it is in dying that we are born to eternal life. Amen.

SCRIPTURE PASSAGES TO CALM YOUR FEARS AND RESTORE YOUR COURAGE

- **1 Peter 3:8:** Finally, all of you, have unity of spirit, sympathy, love of the brethren, a tender heart and a humble mind.
- **Philippians 2:2:** Complete my joy by being of the same mind, having the same love, being in full accord and of one mind.

- **Colossians 3:14:** Above all these put on love, which binds everything together in perfect harmony.

WORDS OF WISDOM AND ENCOURAGEMENT

- "In what is necessary, unity; in what is not necessary, liberty; and in all things charity." —St. Augustine of Hippo
- "Unity does not imply uniformity; it does not necessarily mean doing everything together or thinking in the same way. Nor does it signify a loss of identity. Unity in diversity is actually the opposite: it involves the joyful recognition and acceptance of the various gifts which the Holy Spirit gives to each one and the placing of these gifts at the service of all members of the Church. It means knowing how to listen, to accept differences, and having the freedom to think differently and express oneself with complete respect toward the other who is my brother or sister. Do not be afraid of differences!" —Pope Francis
- "Act in such a way that all those who come in contact with you will go away joyful. Sow happiness about you because you have received much from God; give, then, generously to others. They should take leave of you with their hearts filled with joy, even if they have no more than touched the hem of your garment." —St. Faustina Kowalska
- "The world knows that Catholics have a high standard of purity. But the world is not going to be impressed unless it is assured that Catholics keep it." —Ronald Knox

RESOURCES FOR VIRTUAL MASSES, ADORATION, AND PRAYERS

- **Ave Maria Radio:** www.avemariaradio.net
- **EWTN:** Daily Mass: 8 a.m., noon, 7 p.m., and midnight (Eastern Time) and on YouTube
- EWTN daily spiritual helps (check program schedule), including the Rosary, Divine Mercy and St. Michael Chaplets, Pope Francis's daily private Mass, teaching videos, movies, and much more. See also EWTN's extensive online Catholicism information and its YouTube archive of many programs.
- **Daily Mass with Bishop Robert Barron:** www.WordOnFire.org
- **Live Adoration:** www.ewtn.com/catholicism/adoration
- **Virtual Adoration online:** virtualadoration.home.blog
- Check your local parish or diocese for churches that livestream Masses and Divine Mercy Chaplets.
- **How to find a Catholic church near you:** www.MassTimes.org
- **Diocese locator:** www.usccb.org/about/bishops-and-dioceses/diocesan-locator.cfm
- **Light a candle online:** redemptoristsdenver.org/light-a-candle
- **Request prayers from nuns online:** epicpew.com/know-can-request-prayers-nuns-online
- **Requests prayers from Passionist nuns:** www.passionistnuns.org/prayer-request

RESOURCES FOR SPIRITUAL GUIDANCE

- **USCCB resources for Catholics during COVID-19:** www.usccb.org/about/communications/usccb-president-reflection-and-prayer-during-coronavirus.cfm
- **Archbishop Allen Vigneron, "10 Guideposts for Christians in the Time of the Coronavirus Pandemic,"** *Detroit Catholic*: detroitcatholic.com/voices/archbishop-allen-h-vigneron/10-guideposts-for-christians-in-the-time-of-the-coronavirus-pandemic
- **Prayer in the Time of the Coronavirus,** Archbishop José H. Gomez, Los Angeles: sacredheartsisters.com/wp-content/uploads/2020/03/Our-Lady-of-Guadalupe.pdf
- **St. John Vianney, patron saint of parish priests:** www.ewtn.com/catholicism/saints/john-vianney-653

PRIESTS ONLINE TO HELP GUIDE
YOU ON YOUR WAY

- **Fr. Mike Schmitz,** Ascension Presents: www.youtube.com/ascensionpresents
- **Msgr. Charles Pope:** www.msgrpope.com
- **Fr. John Riccardo:** actsxxix.org/media/resources/
- **Fr. Frank Pavone, Priests for Life:** www.PriestsforLife.org
- **Bishop Robert Barron:** www.WordOnFire.org
- **Fr. Donald Calloway:** www.fathercalloway.com/

HELP FOR
LEADERS IN GOVERNMENT,
COMMUNITY, AND THE MEDIA

Working Together, You Make a Tremendous Difference

It takes courage and some pretty thick skin to do what you do in general. Now let's throw having to deal with a worldwide pandemic into the mix. Having spent more than twenty years in the rough-and-tumble news business, and having interviewed countless public servants and government officials, I can attest to the fact that being in the public spotlight is extremely demanding and often a thankless job as well. Sometimes you're under pressure to pay attention to agendas and politics instead of what's right, and it may seem, on any given day, that you just can't do right by anyone, especially when developments in addressing the coronavirus crisis change by the minute.

Never forget that you a play a crucial role in serving public health and safety. The Lord has you, as St. Teresa of Avila says, right where you need to be. We need your gifts, strengths, and talents, tools that can guide us on to better days. Take heart and call on God to help you stand your ground.

HELPFUL THINGS YOU CAN DO

- Pray *for* your co-workers in the government and media. Pray for the wisdom and the courage to make good decisions concerning actions needed to address the virus, as well as the disseminating of important information.

- Offer to pray *with* your co-workers. You might be surprised at just how open they might be. A Christian anchorwoman in my hometown was often looked down upon for her strong faith. That was until there was a workplace shooting at their TV station. Suddenly, as she later explained to me, she was humbled and pleasantly surprised that her co-workers sought her advice and welcomed her offers to pray for and with them.

- Stay connected to your family, friends, and, most importantly, God. Despite the intensity of your work, no one can be "on" 24/7. You need balance, especially when you're faced with making important decisions that impact so many.

- As busy as you may be, try to find some time during your day, even if just a few minutes, away from the hustle and bustle. Newsrooms and government offices are filled with noise and more noise. God comes to us in silence, or in a "still, small voice," as the Old Testament tells us (1 Kings 19:12).

- Keep a journal—not to add one more thing to your already packed schedule, but because jotting down brief thoughts, experiences, and prayers can be very cathartic. It will also ensure that you'll have pages full of reflections and memories that will provide some guidance and encouragement in the future.

PRAYERS FOR PEACE AND CONSOLATION

Prayer for Our Leaders

God of power and might, wisdom and justice, through You authority is rightly administered, laws are enacted, and judgment is decreed. Assist with Your spirit of counsel and fortitude the president and other government leaders of the United States. May they always seek the ways of righteousness, justice, and mercy. Grant that they may be enabled by Your powerful protection to lead our country with honesty and integrity. We ask this through Christ our Lord.

Prayer for Mass-Media Workers

Lord God Almighty, we bow our heads in thanksgiving because You have given us the grace to spread the Good News about You and about the good things happening to us. Through print, radio, and television, You placed us here to be instruments of the good by telling the truth, not in any way to injure others through word or deed. Please send us the Holy Spirit to guide us and inspire us to do only the good to our fellow men and to guide them closer to You. Protect us from the temptation to use our positions of power to destroy the reputation of others. Instead, help us to be instruments of peace and love so that the world will be a better place to live in. This we ask through Jesus Christ, our Lord. Amen.

SCRIPTURE PASSAGES TO CALM YOUR FEARS AND RESTORE YOUR COURAGE

- **John 6:20:** It is I; do not be afraid.
- **John 8:32:** You will know the truth, and the truth will make you free.
- **1 John 3:18:** Little children, let us not love in word or speech but in deed and in truth.
- **1 John 1:6:** If we say we have fellowship with him while we walk in darkness, we lie and do not live according to the truth.
- **Philippians 4:8:** Finally, brethren, whatever is true, whatever is honorable, whatever is just, whatever is pure, whatever is lovely, whatever is gracious, if there is any excellence, if there is anything worthy of praise, think about these things.
- **Proverbs 10:32:** The lips of the righteous know what is acceptable, but the mouth of the wicked, what is perverse.

WORDS OF WISDOM AND ENCOURAGEMENT

- "The truth is not always the same as the majority decision." —St. John Paul II
- "It is easy to find truth, though it is hard to face it, and harder still to follow it." —Archbishop Fulton Sheen
- "The truth is the truth even if no one believes it, and a lie is a lie even if everyone believes it." —Archbishop Fulton Sheen

- "If there is something more excellent than the truth, then that is God; if not, then truth itself is God." — St. Augustine of Hippo
- "The truth does not change according to our ability to stomach it." — Flannery O'Connor

RESOURCES

- **How to find/contact your government officials or get government help:** www.usa.gov/elected-officials
- **St. Thomas More, patron saint of civil servants and government employees:** www.ewtn.com/catholicism/saints/thomas-more-787
- **St. Thomas More, patron saint of statesmen and politicians:** www.ewtn.com/catholicism/library/saint-thomas-more-patron-of-statesmen-and-politicians-8319
- **Archangels Gabriel, Raphael, and Michael, patron saints of communications:** www.franciscanmissionaries.com/2681-2/
- **WhiteHouse.gov:** www.whitehouse.gov
- **U.S. coronavirus government website:** www.coronavirus.gov
- **Epic Pew:** www.epicpew.com
- **Catholic Exchange:** www.catholicexchange.com
- **Eternal Word Television Network:** www.ewtn.com
- **_Our Sunday Visitor_:** www.OSVNews.com
- **_National Catholic Register_:** www.NCRegister.com
- **Catholic News Agency:** www.CatholicNewsAgency.com

- **Vatican News:** www.vaticannews.va/en.html
- **Patti Maguire Armstrong:** http://www.pattimaguire-armstrong.com/
- **Teresa Tomeo blog:** https://teresatomeo.com/category/blog/
- **Women of Grace:** www.WomenofGrace.com
- **Aleteia:** www.Aleteia.org
- **Patheos Catholic:** www.patheos.com/catholic
- **Catholic Spiritual Direction:** www.SpiritualDirection.com
- **Ave Maria Radio:** www.avemariaradio.net

12

Your Devotional for These Times of Pestilence

No, in all these things we are more than
conquerors through him who loved us.

—Romans 8:37

DAILY PRAYERS

Sign of the Cross
In the name of the Father, and of the Son,
and of the Holy Spirit. Amen.

Our Father
Our Father, who art in Heaven, hallowed be Thy name;
Thy Kingdom come; Thy will be done on earth as it is in
Heaven. Give us this day our daily bread; and forgive us our
trespasses as we forgive those who trespass against us; and lead
us not into temptation, but deliver us from evil. Amen.

Glory Be
Glory be to the Father, and to the Son, and to the
Holy Spirit; as it was in the beginning, is now, and
ever shall be, world without end. Amen.

Three-Second Daily Prayer
Sunday (for spiritual growth): *Holy Spirit, Sanctifier*
of souls, grace our souls with the holiness of God.

Monday (for world peace): *Prince of Peace, bring true*
peace to persons, families, and nations everywhere.

Tuesday (for the homeless): *Jesus, You were born homeless.*
Have pity on all without shelter or warmth today.

Wednesday (for the physically and emotionally ill): *Heal*
all the sick, Lord, who are suffering in body, mind, or spirit.

Thursday (for abused children): *Comfort Your little ones, Jesus, who are abused in mind or body. Heal them.*

Friday (for the chemically addicted): *By Your thirst on the Cross, Jesus, normalize all disordered cravings.*

Saturday (for vocations): *Lord of the harvest, send many holy and concerned laborers into your vineyard.*

Jesus Prayer
*Lord Jesus, Son of the living God,
have mercy on me, a sinner.*

Prayer of Spiritual Communion
(if You Can't Attend Mass or Receive Holy Communion)
My Jesus, I believe that You are present in the Most Holy Sacrament. I love You above all things, and I desire to receive You into my soul. Since I cannot at this moment receive You sacramentally, come at least spiritually into my heart. I embrace You as if You were already there and unite myself wholly to You. Never permit me to be separated from You. Amen.

Act of Contrition
My God, I am sorry for my sins with all my heart. In choosing to do wrong and failing to do good, I have sinned against You, whom I should love above all things. I firmly intend, with Your help, to do penance, to sin no more, and to avoid whatever leads me to sin. Our Savior Jesus Christ suffered and died for us. In His name, my God, have mercy.

For Confidence in Prayer

*O Jesus, Your disciples often found You at prayer, and so
they asked You to teach them how to do it. Help me to pray in
confidence to the Father, just as You did. When I am facing my
own agony of doubt and fear, pray with me so that I may find
courage and hope. When my life leads me to the cross, take
my hand so that my heart stays strong. Most of all, strengthen
my resolve to pray: Not my will, but Yours be done. Amen.*

Review of Your Day

This is a version of the five-step Daily Examen that St. Ignatius
practiced.

1. Become aware of God's presence.
2. Review the day with gratitude.
3. Pay attention to your emotions.
4. Choose one feature of the day and pray from it.
5. Look toward tomorrow.

PRAYERS TO ACCEPT GOD'S WILL

Serenity Prayer

*God, grant me the serenity to accept the things I
cannot change, the courage to change the things that
I can, and the wisdom to know the difference.*

Prayer of St. Francis

*Lord, make me an instrument of Your peace; where there is
hatred, let me sow love; where there is injury, pardon; where
there is doubt, faith; where there is despair, hope; where there is
darkness, light; and where there is sadness, joy. Divine Master,
grant that I may not so much seek to be consoled as to console; to
be understood, as to understand; to be loved, as to love; for it is
in giving that we receive, it is in pardoning that we are pardoned,
and it is in dying that we are born to eternal life. Amen.*

Prayers to Be Mindful of God's Presence

*Lord Jesus Christ, You said to your disciples, "I am with you
always." Be with me today, as I offer myself to You. Hear my
prayers for others and for myself, and keep me in Your care.*

> *Christ be with me, Christ within me,*
> *Christ behind me, Christ before me,*
> *Christ beside me, Christ to win me,*
> *Christ to comfort and restore me.*
> *Christ beneath me, Christ above me,*
> *Christ in quiet, Christ in danger,*
> *Christ in hearts of all that love me,*
> *Christ in mouth of friend and stranger.*
> (from St. Patrick's Breastplate)

*O gracious and holy Father, give us wisdom to perceive You,
diligence to seek You, patience to wait for You, eyes to behold You,
a heart to meditate upon You, and a life to proclaim You, through
the power of the Spirit of Jesus Christ our Lord.* (St. Benedict)

Prayers for Healing
Gracious Lord, remember in Your mercy those who suffer today. Give strength and encouragement to those who minister to their needs. Remember Your promise not to let them be tested beyond what they are able to bear. Above all, give them the reassurance that You are with them as they walk through this valley of the shadows of death. And in Your good time, send healing of body and spirit. In Jesus' name. Amen.

Father, Your Son accepted our sufferings to teach us the virtue of patience in human illness. Hear the prayers we offer for our sick brother/sister. May all who suffer pain, illness, or disease realize that they have been chosen to be saints and know that they are joined to Christ in His suffering for the salvation of the world. We ask this through Christ our Lord. Amen.

Prayers for the Dying
Almighty and merciful God, who has bestowed on mankind saving remedies and the gift of everlasting life, look graciously upon us Your servants and comfort the souls You have made, that, in the hour of their passing, cleansed from all stain of sin, they may deserve to be presented to You, their Creator, by the hands of the holy angels. Through Christ our Lord. Amen.

Prayer for a Peaceful Death
All praise and glory are Yours, Lord our God, for You have called us to serve You in love. Bless all who have grown old in Your service, and give N. strength and courage to continue to follow Jesus, Your Son. We ask this through Christ our Lord. Amen.

Prayer at the Time of Death
*Go forth, Christian soul, from this world in the name of
God, the almighty Father, who created you, in the name of
Jesus Christ, Son of the living God, who suffered for you, in
the name of the Holy Spirit, who was poured out upon you.
Go forth, faithful Christian. May you live in peace this day,
may your home be with God in Zion, with Mary, the virgin
Mother of God, with Joseph, and all the angels and saints.*

SCRIPTURE PASSAGES FOR THE SICK AND THE DYING

- **Psalm 23:4:** Even though I walk through the valley of the shadow of death, I fear no evil; for thou art with me; thy rod and thy staff, they comfort me.
- **John 11:25–26:** Jesus said ..., "I am the resurrection and the life. Whoever believes in me, though he die, yet shall he live, and everyone who lives and believes in me shall never die."
- **John 3:16:** For God so loved the world, that he gave his only Son, that whoever believes in him should not perish but have eternal life.
- **Romans 8:35:** What will separate us from the love of Christ? (NABRE)
- **Romans 14:8:** If we live, we live to the Lord, and if we die, we die to the Lord; so then, whether we live or whether we die, we are the Lord's.
- **1 Thessalonians 4:17:** We shall always be with the Lord.

- **Psalm 31:5:** Into thy hand I commit my spirit. (cf. Luke 23:46)
- **Acts 7:59:** Lord Jesus, receive my spirit.
- **Revelation 21:4:** He will wipe away every tear from their eyes, and death shall be no more, neither shall there be mourning nor crying nor pain any more.

HOW TO MAKE A GOOD CONFESSION

Prayer before Confession

O most merciful God! Prostrate at Your feet, I implore Your forgiveness. I sincerely desire to leave all my evil ways and to confess my sins with all sincerity to You and to Your priest. I am a sinner; have mercy on me, O Lord. Give me a lively faith and a firm hope in the Passion of my Redeemer. Give me, for Your mercy's sake, a sorrow for having offended so good a God. Mary, my mother, refuge of sinners, pray for me that I may make a good confession. Amen.

- Do an examination of conscience (see below).
- Tell your sins simply and honestly. You might even want to say out loud the circumstances and the root causes of your sins and ask the priest for advice or direction.
- Say the Act of Contrition.

Act of Contrition

My God, I am sorry for my sins with all my heart. In choosing to do wrong and failing to do good, I have sinned against

You, whom I should love above all things. I firmly intend,
with Your help, to do penance, to sin no more, and to avoid
whatever leads me to sin. Our Savior Jesus Christ suffered
and died for us. In His name, my God, have mercy.

- Spend some time in prayer with God, thanking and praising Him for the gift of His mercy.

IF YOU ARE NOT ABLE TO CONFESS TO A PRIEST IN PERSON

When contrition arises from pure love of God, it is called perfect contrition. Such contrition remits venial sins; it also obtains forgiveness of mortal sins if it includes the firm resolution to receive as soon as possible sacramental confession by a priest.

Examination of Conscience based on
the Ten Commandments (by the USCCB)

1. I am the Lord your God. You shall not have strange gods before me.
   - Do I give God time every day in prayer?
   - Do I seek to love Him with my whole heart?
   - Have I been involved with superstitious practices or with the occult?
   - Do I seek to surrender myself to God's Word as taught by the Church?
   - Have I ever received Communion in the state of mortal sin?
   - Have I ever deliberately told a lie in Confession, or have I withheld a mortal sin from the priest in Confession?
   - Are there other "gods" in my life? Money, security, power, people, and so forth?

2. You shall not take the name of the Lord your God in vain.
   - Have I used God's name in vain—lightly or carelessly?
   - Have I been angry with God?
   - Have I wished evil upon any other person?
   - Have I insulted a sacred person or abused a sacred object?

3. Remember to keep holy the Lord's Day.
   - Have I deliberately missed Mass on Sundays or holy days of obligation?
   - Have I tried to observe Sunday as a family day and a day of rest?
   - Do I do needless work on Sunday?

4. Honor your father and your mother.
   - Do I honor and obey my parents?
   - Have I neglected my duties to my spouse and children?
   - Have I given my family good religious example?
   - Do I try to bring peace into my home life?
   - Do I care for my aged and infirm relatives?

5. You shall not kill.
   - Have I had an abortion or encouraged or helped anyone to have an abortion?
   - Have I physically harmed anyone?
   - Have I abused alcohol or drugs?
   - Did I give scandal to anyone, thereby leading him or her into sin?
   - Have I been angry or resentful?
   - Have I harbored hatred in my heart?
   - Have I mutilated myself through any form of sterilization?
   - Have I encouraged or condoned sterilization?

- Have I engaged, in any way, in sins against human life, such as artificial insemination or in vitro fertilization?
- Have I participated in or approved of euthanasia?

6. You shall not commit adultery.
   - Have I been faithful to my marriage vows in thought and action?
   - Have I engaged in any sexual activity outside of marriage?
   - Have I used any method of contraception or artificial birth control in my marriage?
   - Has each sexual act in my marriage been open to the transmission of new life?
   - Have I been guilty of masturbation?
   - Do I seek to control my thoughts and imagination?
   - Have I respected all members of the opposite sex, or have I thought of other people as mere objects?
   - Have I been guilty of any homosexual activity?
   - Do I seek to be chaste in my thoughts, words, and actions?
   - Am I careful to dress modestly?

7. You shall not steal.
   - Have I stolen what is not mine?
   - Have I returned or made restitution for what I have stolen?
   - Do I waste time at work, at school, and at home?
   - Do I gamble excessively, thereby denying my family their needs?
   - Do I pay my debts promptly?
   - Do I seek to share what I have with the poor?
   - Have I cheated anyone out of what is justly his or hers; for example creditors, insurance companies, or big corporations?

8. You shall not bear false witness against your neighbor.
   - Have I lied?
   - Have I gossiped?
   - Do I speak badly of others behind their backs?
   - Am I sincere in my dealings with others?
   - Am I critical, negative, or uncharitable in my thoughts of others?
   - Do I keep secret what should be kept confidential?
   - Have I injured the reputation of others by slander?

9. You shall not desire your neighbor's wife.
   - Have I consented to impure thoughts?
   - Have I caused such thoughts by impure reading, movies, television, the Internet, conversation, or curiosity?
   - Do I pray at once to banish impure thoughts and temptations?
   - Have I behaved in an inappropriate way with members of the opposite sex by flirting, being superficial, and so forth?

10. You shall not desire your neighbor's goods.
    - Am I jealous of what other people have?
    - Do I envy the families or possessions of others?
    - Am I greedy or selfish?
    - Are material possessions the purpose of my life?

acknowledgments

SPECIAL THANKS TO THE amazing rock-star team at Sophia Institute Press who all have true hearts for evangelization. They dropped everything to help this book get published and printed in just two weeks from conception to publication. I want to first thank Charlie McKinney for his unwavering support of this project of evangelization and especially for his flexibility and openness to this book idea, including translating it into other languages. I am particularly impressed with how his team work together so unified with "all hands on deck" and their willingness to accommodate at every turn.

Thanks also to the fabulous Sophia editorial team—John Barger and Nora Malone—for their expertise and for giving up their Holy Week and Triduum to edit this book into a published work.

Special thanks to Tom Allen and his amazing Sophia marketing team—Sarah Lemieux, Molly Rublee, and all who helped with the beautiful cover design and marketing materials—as well as special thanks to Alysha Daley and Sheila Perry for working with such a quick turnaround.

I especially want to thank Gail Coniglio, my literary agent and publicist, for her tireless round-the-clock work on this book to help with editing, cover design, and invaluable insights and marketing ideas for evangelization. And thanks to my marketing support, Marcy Klatt, for helping to gather the many resources and prayers we included here. I also want to thank all the members of the amazing "T Team" that I collaborate with—Gail Coniglio, Marcy Klatt, Palma Poochigian, Patti Armstrong, Vanessa Denha Garmo, and Jeff Cann—who helped keep all of the other evangelization projects running smoothly while I was writing this book. I could never have written this book without them.

I want to also give a special shout out to all those who endorsed the book: Fr. John Riccardo; Fr. Chris Alar, MIC; Kathryn Jean Lopez; Al Kresta; and Susan Tassone, all who were willing to carve out precious time during Holy Week and work on our pressing deadline.

Last, but not least, thank you to my wonderful husband, Deacon Dom, for his unwavering support and love for evangelization.

about the author

Teresa Tomeo is an author, syndicated Catholic talk-show host, and motivational speaker with more than thirty years of experience in TV, radio, and newspaper. She spent nineteen of those years working in front of a camera as a reporter and anchor in the Detroit market.

In 2000, Teresa left the secular media to start her own speaking and communications company, Teresa Tomeo Communications, LLC, and her website and blog (TeresaTomeo.com). Her daily morning radio program, *Catholic Connection*, is produced by Ave Maria Radio and EWTN's Global Catholic Radio Network and can be heard on over five hundred domestic and international AM and FM radio affiliates worldwide, including SiriusXM Satellite Radio. Over the past two decades, Teresa has traveled extensively throughout Italy and has led pilgrimages and tours there more than fifty times. In 2019, she founded *T's Italy*, a travel consultation company, along with its website (TravelItalyExpert.com), where she shares insider tips for where to eat, stay, shop, and play in that beautiful country.

To learn about more future books by Teresa published by Sophia Institute Press, please visit: www.SophiaInstitute.com/Teresa.

Sophia Institute

Sophia Institute is a nonprofit institution that seeks to nurture the spiritual, moral, and cultural life of souls and to spread the Gospel of Christ in conformity with the authentic teachings of the Roman Catholic Church.

Sophia Institute Press fulfills this mission by offering translations, reprints, and new publications that afford readers a rich source of the enduring wisdom of mankind.

Sophia Institute also operates the popular online resource CatholicExchange.com. *Catholic Exchange* provides world news from a Catholic perspective as well as daily devotionals and articles that will help readers to grow in holiness and live a life consistent with the teachings of the Church.

In 2013, Sophia Institute launched Sophia Institute for Teachers to renew and rebuild Catholic culture through service to Catholic education. With the goal of nurturing the spiritual, moral, and cultural life of souls, and an abiding respect for the role and work of teachers, we strive to provide materials and programs that are at once enlightening to the mind and ennobling to the heart; faithful and complete, as well as useful and practical.

Sophia Institute gratefully recognizes the Solidarity Association for preserving and encouraging the growth of our apostolate over the course of many years. Without their generous and timely support, this book would not be in your hands.

www.SophiaInstitute.com
www.CatholicExchange.com
www.SophiaInstituteforTeachers.org

Sophia Institute Press® is a registered trademark of Sophia Institute.
Sophia Institute is a tax-exempt institution as defined by the
Internal Revenue Code, Section 501(c)(3). Tax ID 22-2548708.